LORD COLTRANE

LOVE Avatar

UNLEASH YOUR DIVINE FEMININE SUPERPOWERS
& AWAKEN THE GODDESS WITHIN

ISBN: 978-19-5-315324-1

Published by

If you are interested in publishing through Lifestyle Entrepreneurs Press,
write to: *Publishing@LifestyleEntrepreneursPress.com*

Publications or foreign rights acquisition of our catalog books.
Learn More: *www.LifestyleEntrepreneursPress.com*

Printed in the USA

LOVE Avatar

Unleash Your Divine Feminine Superpowers
and Awaken the Goddess Within

LORD COLTRANE

To the light in every soul and the love in every heart. May your light and love spread like a virus and infect everyone you touch.

Vision quest: a journey into the
sacredness of your soul...

Contents

Love Avatar

Hey, Soul Sister!

"There is a vitality, a life force, an energy, a quickening that is translated through you into action, and because there is only one of you in all of time, this expression is unique. And if you block it, it will never exist through any other medium and it will be lost. The world will not have it. It is not your business to determine how good it is, nor how valuable, nor how it compares with other expressions. It is your business to keep it yours clearly and directly, to keep the channels open."
—Martha Graham

Hey, soul sister! I just want to take a moment right now to acknowledge you. Your beauty, your wisdom, your light, your love. You are the most exquisite thing on this planet, and in this Universe. I'll share with you why this is true, and why this truth matters.

You possess an inner cauldron of unique magical powers and talents bursting to be set free. You contain a light so brilliant and beautiful that once unleashed it can never be forgotten. The chalice in your heart is filled with the nectar of the Goddess, and once it begins to overflow and spread, you will leave drops of liquid love everywhere you go.

You may not know it yet, but you are an electric power that creates the moons and the stars and the planets. You are equally a magnetic force that attracts and holds solar systems and galaxies together. Your body has a genius all its own, independent of the critical mind, that holds divine wisdom waiting for you to harness. You have the ability to create *anything* your magical mind can imagine, and in the most phenomenal of ways.

You have desires.

You have a significant purpose.

Your individual spark of mysterious life force is dancing with the energies of the Divine. The goddesses from the archetypal realms are dying to express themselves with you and through you. *All* of Creation wants to be fed by the sacredness of your experiences, good and bad.

I invite you to inhale this Truth...and then exhale any ridiculous doubts about it.

We desperately need more beauty and light and love in this world. We desperately need *your* beauty, *your* light, and *your* love in this world. I am not talking about the superficial kind of beauty, or ego spotlights, or soulless connection. I am talking about an energy that ignites the passion for higher evolution, the kind that uplifts humanity and brings in more peace, love, and bliss.

What would you do with this kind of power? Who would you become?

You, my soul sister, are part of the love brigade, whose mission, if you choose to take it, is to unleash your unique feminine superpowers, and to spread your unique gifts in this world with a passion and purpose that inspires others...in your own way, of course. Your "job" is to learn to create your own reality instead of being dragged, kicking and screaming, in the direction of someone else's ideas of you. From here, you call in soul love and soul purpose.

How do I know? Because I'm one of the Sacred Rebels here to help shake things up. Sacred Rebels are passionate and pioneering souls who are here to help liberate divine feminine energy, like the energy that lurks deep within your soul, so that together we inspire a glorious world, personal and collective, to live in. Some of us were born with this creative and spunky spirit to inspire an individually authentic life, while others have chosen to join us for the freedom it brings. This is not an exclusive group; it is an open and inclusive family that you are welcome to be a part of anytime.

If you are reading these words right now, we are soul connected. We have been summoned together by the golden karmic thread, created by the Goddess Mother herself, that dangles from the great tapestry of Life. She is asking us to awaken to our individual inner goddess so that we can create a new reality for ourselves, to reach our highest potential as women, to know who we really are, and to do our part to nourish everything on Earth. From this exalted place on the throne of Being, we can do more, create more, love more, and thrive more.

This is our birthright. This is necessary for the transformation from a patriarchal society of competition, oppression, separation, blame, shame, right, and wrong, to a conscious society of collaboration, equanimity, connection, radical acceptance, kindness, and non-judgment. At the very least, this awakening of your divine feminine essence is simply about living your bliss.

This process of becoming, however, requires the reclaiming and unshaming of the lost and forbidden parts that make us whole, so we remember our innermost desires. We must follow our pleasure, do what sets our souls on fire, and simply allow our truest nature to reveal herself. I promise, the moment you meet the real you,

3

you will understand the poetry of Rumi, the sounds of the cosmos, and the dance of the Divine. This is love.

What do you say, shall we be friends?

{Lesson: You are part of the Love Brigade. This is Truth.}

CHAPTER 1

The Mystery of You

The Way of the Goddess

> "The Goddess doesn't enter us from outside;
> she emerges from deep within. She is
> not held back by what happened in the
> past. She is conceived in consciousness,
> born in love, and nurtured by higher
> thinking. She is integrity and value,
> created and sustained by the hard work
> of personal growth and the discipline
> of a life lived actively in hope."
> —Marianne Williamson

What if every single hardship that has ever happened *to* you was actually happening *for* you? What if these difficult moments were the perfect makers of Kings and Queens that you *chose* to experience so that you could embody self-sovereignty in this lifetime? What if you were supposed to master these lessons so that you could clear all your "bad karma" and begin co-creating with the Universe? What if you have been guided in this way toward loving and being loved in an epic way? What if you knew this led to finding bliss in everything you do, or finding a passion and a purpose that fulfilled every aspect of your being? What if every single synchronicity was perfectly orchestrated to lead you to this very moment?

This is the way of the Goddess.

She understands that she is the Creatrix of her own destiny, has written her story of redemption and reclamation before she even entered the Earth plane, and has learned to unleash her feminine superpowers to experience the life and love she deserves.

I don't believe in coincidences. Since you are reading these words, it is a Cosmic sign there is something *more* for you; something deeper, more expansive, richer, and more textured than this 3D world can ever express. This "something" lies buried beneath the surface, and is desperate to be unleashed to its fullest, most potent, most radiant, most magnificent potential. This "thing" is your soul, your soul's longing to reconnect with an incomprehensibly brilliant power that is both electric and magnetic. This something is you – not just the regular you, but the divine you.

Let me explain.

Your body is the Holy Grail that holds your magic. In order for us to reconnect to this magic, we must overcome the shames and ruptures we've had to endure in life, and successfully transform them into art and meaningful purpose. This will bring you to a place of truly knowing yourself, not just your one Self, but your *many* Selves. We are multifaceted beings with a multidimensional essence. When we tap into this power, it is an energy that cannot be ignored; is an energy that creates; it is an energy that heals and regenerates; it is an energy that attracts all your desires; it is an energy that can change the world for the better. The ancient texts use the term "the Goddess of Countless Names and Faces" to describe the fullness of an unleashed, untamed, and awakened woman. Trust me, it feels really yummy to be this type of woman, to come home to your own divinity.

To reveal your soul is a process of unveiling, transforming, creating, and witnessing. To experience her is to experience *all* of you. The byproduct of this "becoming" is beyond beauty, it's pure radiance. It's not just confidence, it's radical self-love. It's more than sexy, it's a sacred intimacy and a love affair with the completeness of yourself. This kind of woman doesn't just call in lasting love or even recreate the love she's had, *she is love in the flesh*.

You and I, along with the collective, have a yearning to wake up to the ancient mysteries of the goddesses, to discover how to tap into the spiritual wisdom of the feminine, and to understand why we feel such a strong pull toward an awakening of this kind. Somehow we 'know,' but have no idea what exactly we know, or why we want to know it. We are being led to something, but have no idea how to listen to the messages or read the signs to feel *truly* empowered, confident, connected, loved, and worthy. This book is your guide to that wisdom.

Many women are still stuck in a mundane definition of what feminine empowerment means, mostly because it is defined from a masculine perspective, which can be confusing. We are taught to value presentational beauty, or money, or degrees, or a specific type of mothering. Note that I say "or," not "and." We are not allowed to be *all* things from this patriarchal worldview. So we focus on the superficial successes, just to make sense of things. Let's change this, shall we?

Life is messy. Love is messy. Our very human needs – to be seen, heard, and understood; to be accepted for who we truly are at our core; to be appreciated and noticed for our unique talents and contributions in the world; and to experience affection and belonging – are distorted into a superficial perfection and connection, thus distorting what it means to be an empowered woman in today's culture.

We have ignored the devastating beauty of our pains and vulnerabilities, the abundance of love we can learn from a world of

8

diversity, the simple life lessons of kindness and presence, the elegant genius of nature's constant unfolding, and the incredible experience of taking the profound journey through the depths of our souls.

To be divinely feminine doesn't simply mean to soften and surrender away from our learned masculine masks, as some men would prefer. It is to embody the range of the feminine: the dark, the light, the wild, the tame, the fierce, the tender, the grit, and the grace. It is to see the world from a broader, more compassionate, more collaborative perspective. There aren't enough empowered feminine role models to share the true wisdom of the Goddess, and we are in a crucial time where we need many more beings, the masses of evolved women *and* men, to awaken to this knowledge in order to usher in a new age of evolution. I hope you will be one of them.

What we do have to help us are the mystery teachings of the divine feminine exemplified by ancient goddess philosophies across the globe. We have the ability to tap into the archetypal realm of Creative Consciousness, where it is said that the gods and goddesses are waiting to express themselves through us. No longer is it necessary to sit in isolation in a cave on top of a mountain to find enlightenment. No longer does it apply to follow just one lineage of teachings. When you tap into the goddess energies, you tap into oneness and the field of infinite potential and possibilities. More and more people are "waking up" by spontaneous activation, which is what happened to me. Do not get me wrong, to have a spontaneous spiritual awakening is not for the faint of heart. The stages are non-linear and intense. You might experience what you think is the darkest night of your soul, only to melt into the beauty of connection with All That Is, and then back again into the darkness. The awakening of your Kundalini power can be hard on the body. Regardless, every single one of us has access to this very potent and magical spiritual energy, you just have to allow it to arise.

Aren't you curious to know what flavor of goddess has been trying to work with you? Aren't you curious to know what your various selves have to say? And once we individuate the parts of you to get to your core essence, don't you want to know what you have come here to learn, how your higher self wants to serve? Do you want to meet your soul's love counterpart? To allow this merging of the superficial personalities and the spiritual personalities is to liberate yourself into a higher awareness of what it means to be a multidimensional and multisensory spirit in a human body.

Like all major clean-up projects though, we first have to do a lot of unpacking to see what we want to keep or toss, and it is never a tidy process. Some of us have to dive into the swamp and meet the mudslingers, others have to descend the layers of Hell to confront the Devil himself. The lucky ones simply have to let go and forgive, but that isn't easy either. It takes incredible resilience and surrender to look past superficialities and look inward for answers to some very profound questions, like: *Who am I at my core? What is my soul's deepest desire? What is my purpose? What am I truly grateful for?*

Sometimes our old wounds of unworthiness, rejection, shame, betrayal, and loss prevent us from actually accessing our own truth, and becoming the highest potential of being. The greatest thing you will discover once you do this, though, is the truth that these trials are actually treasures that reveal your most unique superpowers and the real you. I invite you now to take a meditative moment to open up to your full senses to experience the subtleties that surround you, because we have some very exciting exploring to do together.

{Lesson: The Way of the Goddess is happening for you right now.}

I Desire

I'll tell you mine, if you tell me yours...

I'm talking about your deepest and darkest and most secret desires. The ones that you might be repressing just in case you think someone can read your mind, or your heart. Most women don't ever think about their desires at all. Some feel guilty, selfish, undeserving, or were never given permission to have them. But what do you really want? What do you desire at your deepest, deepest core level?

Let's practice...

> {*Take a moment right now (don't hesitate!) to write down a few desires here in the margins, or say them out loud, or get out your notebook and start a desire journal. Do this now! Put a date on it, and then we'll get back to it for more refinement.*}

We all deserve to have our deepest desires met, to feel connected, alive, radiant, free, and fulfilled. I assure you, desires are the seeds that create our luscious Gardens of Eden, Paradises Found, and Heavens on Earth.

I know what you are thinking: if desires were that easy, there would already be peace on Earth, no loneliness, no poverty, no breakups, no destruction of the planet, no bullies. There would only be love, beauty, kindness, compassion, abundance, and more love. Some of us might have already been swooped up by Prince

Charming, ravished by a god, been crowned the fairest of them all, or already own a mansion or two in Wonderland. Girls might even run the world by now.

The word "desire" often gets muddled up in the sexual, self-serving, or shallow needs of humans, especially if we are still in the unconscious level of being. At this unconscious, or 3D level, we are focused on the superficial wants, like more money, a set of trivial conditions for our romantic partner, a certain lifestyle, a different job.

The problem is, most of us don't actually know what we desire for ourselves, because we don't know our full self yet. We fall into the trap of hoping to make others happy, especially with our families and intimate relationships, so in turn we think they will make us happy. This is a very passive-aggressive way to love, requiring others to change, not ourselves. We end up searching for happiness outside instead of inside.

I consider myself to be "awakened and aware," but even still, when I was confronted with a desire in my relationship I said to my partner, "the only thing I want is that you love me for who I am." That sounded so elevated and selfless to me. But if I really think about this desire, I was asking my partner to shift in ways he was not ready for at the time.

When we do focus on what we desire for ourselves, we get so specific and myopic that we miss the bigger, more exalted version of what we can manifest. There is definitely power in knowing what you desire, but the secret to the spontaneous fulfillment of our desires is in *how* we desire. Desires need to be positive, aligned with our truest self, laced with gratitude, open for the best outcome, and we must be ready and willing to receive them. So many women who I guide in this process do not realize they aren't yet ready to accept their greatest desires, and their whole lives turn upside down. We will continue to perfect this process, but for now let's practice again...

I have this intense desire to unleash my divine feminine soul; to be magnetic, powerful, deep, spiritual, and so sensually alive.

I desire to be the type of woman who is beyond beautiful, but radiant.

I desire not just confidence, but true radical self-love.

I desire to be way more than sexual; I want to be a Sacred Goddess of love and light who embodies her fullest potential and inspires creativity.

I desire to know my superpowers, and how to use them for good.

I desire to create something meaningful and lasting that will serve others in a soulful way.

I desire constant abundance and beauty to surround me.

I don't just want to call in lasting love, or even recreate my past love experiences. I want to become Love *in the flesh.*

I want to know the unknowable.

I want to know the Divine.

I want it all.

{Lesson: Desires are powerful.}

Faux Feminine

Before we get to the art and intricacies of desire, let's first take a deeper look into who you are, because if you don't know who you are, how do you know what you really want? I've already given you a glimpse, but you have to believe me first. So, who are you...*really*?

> {*Take another moment right now (before you read on!)*
> *to list how you identify yourself. Again, do it here in the*
> *margins, or say them out loud, or get out your notebook and*
> *add them to your journal. We'll get back to this one, too.*}

Most "everyday" women describe themselves by the roles they play, and most choose just one role to comfortably identify with because of social expectations. Mothers, for example, are expected to give up parts of themselves in devotion to their families. Executive women might hold off on love and family, striving for a seat at the success table. Sexually free and expressive women are often vilified. Goddess forbid any of these portrayals merge into one woman; all hell might break loose. Entertainers, actresses, and supermodels are the only ones who *seem* to be allowed to have a bit more range of expression than "regular" women, but that's mostly because our society puts a high value on presentational beauty, money, and fame. This compartmentalization of women leads us to feeling unfulfilled and cut off from the deeper and more important parts of ourselves. Even if we have the best families,

15

the best jobs, and the best love affairs, we are censored and asked to live in boxes that serve others.

The current social system has defined for women what is appropriate for them, how much they are worth, and what standards they must hold themselves to. It has created the faux feminine: the woman who is still caught up in the daily grind and stress of "keeping up" and "getting it right." Even though we have more and more access to information on organic beauty, holistic health, meditation, and spiritual teachings, there are still expectations and rules that keep women small and one-dimensional.

This system is based on a very old paradigm created by a lower level of masculinity that diminishes the power of women. It has been happening for thousands of years. Of the hundreds of women I have worked with, from stay-at-home moms to high-tech executives, every single one of them has experienced being diminished by the opposite sex in subtle and not so subtle ways. This is true from the news accounts of sexual harassment, gender inequality, biased medicine, and the language being used around the globe to keep women as the second sex. The male lens puts women in compartmentalized boxes that keep us stifled and feeling claustrophobic.

Sadly, we have very few role models of an awakened woman who is *all* things: unashamed of her imperfections, her beauty, her body, her magic, her intuition, her nurturing capacity, her vulnerability, her spirituality, her wild, her sensual, her authenticity, her power.

Believing that the outside world has control over us creates a culture of faux feminine women, both unconscious and conscious, who never look inward to where all the answers lie. The unconscious faux feminine has fallen into the trap of needing to be saved, or has adopted a "lack mentality." She sees the world from a patriarchal masculine perspective. This type of woman feels the need to be superficially pretty and stand out from the crowd to be "better than" other women. She feels she must compete with other women to claim her spot on the throne, whichever throne that is for her, be it at work, in romance, or in her friendships. She has learned to manipulate others to navigate her way "to win" the love, the job, the bestie. The unconscious faux feminine will attract the unconscious faux partners and they will try to "complete" each other with condition after tedious shallow condition. This level of faux feminine may think she is happy, but is always working to keep up her image, her social status, and her money. She focuses on quantity versus the quality of life. The five-hundred-billion-dollar beauty industry tries to keep women at this level of being.

The conscious faux feminine, on the other hand, is the woman who knows that all of this is absolute nonsense, but hasn't experienced a fully empowered feminine that she knows exists. She is looking for the gracious, influential, generous, intelligent, radiant, sexy, soulful, tender, courageous, fierce, collaborative, inclusive, and embodied woman to template. Society has shamed the conscious faux feminine into believing she can only be a fraction of her fullest potential. Society makes her believe that if she chooses wealth, she must do it in a way that disempowers others or she must adopt a masculine persona to accomplish success. Society might guilt her into motherhood and tell her to give up all that she is to serve others selflessly and tirelessly, when she knows she can do both. Society doesn't even let her express herself sexually unless she is the supermodel, actress, or popstar mentioned earlier, so she tucks that part neatly away. The conscious faux feminine feels that something is amiss. She is yearning to know what an unleashed, loving, untamed, nurturing, genius, emotive, erotic, successful, and divine all-at-the-same-time whole woman looks and feels like. She plays it safe, because she has to. Even so-called "evolved spiritual souls" get trapped in this category. They don't seem to make room for the merging of the spiritual world with the material world, the superficial with deep soul meaning, or sexuality with spirituality, even though ancient sacred texts would suggest that the integration of all parts of us is a step toward enlightenment.

We have chosen to give in to the power of shame, guilt, and fear to define ourselves in just one dimension, which doesn't feel good to the multifaceted emotional, embodied, mindful, soulful, and spiritual beings that we truly are. We have separated ourselves into very small pieces, and then accepted too small a box for each one. We choose the good girl, the bad girl, the material girl, the smart girl, the magical girl, or the bombshell. We placate a patriarchal insecurity that has an issue with the power of a fully embodied feminine. It's impossible to shine brightly and unapologetically in the world with fragmented pieces. And let's be honest, we are also scared of what we might do with this kind of power.

A disconnection of who we are at the deepest level means that our desires will not match up with our souls' intentions, which will not match the energy we need for manifestation. We remain unfulfilled, stuck, sometimes even hopeless. And so we yearn and hunger for an unknown quality that exists just beyond our senses.

{Lesson: *Faux is for fur, not for Feminine.*}

The Invitation

"The Divine is calling you.

Her sound is like a song of exquisite yearning about a love so deep your body aches to connect.

Can you hear Her?

The Divine has kissed you.

He touches your lips with a subtle magic that delights and tingles your flesh, igniting a heat that sparks memories so delicious it overwhelms your heart.

Can you taste Him?

The Divine is in a dance of cosmic rapture around you, screaming "I love you" to no one in particular and then to everyone. They merge soul-to-soul, heart-to-heart, and skin-to-skin in an explosion of new Realities.

Can you sense Them?

The Divine is obviously in love...with you.

Beautiful, magnetic, magical, powerful, sensual creature of love, the Divine is asking you to reveal yourself as her mirror; to awaken to your power as a sacred rebel; to unleash your superpowers and discover your multifaceted soul, to awaken to your inner goddess and become Love so that you inspire Love on this planet.

Beloved, to be divinely feminine is to be embodied as the Divine.

You are the Divine. Trust this. Own this.

I love you."

This message came to me in a whisper, but it was actually a message meant for you. I received it during a holotropic breathing exercise at a workshop in Santa Fe, New Mexico. Holotropic breathwork is a technique developed by Stanislav Grof, a Czech psychiatrist and LSD pioneer, to explore higher states of consciousness (or psychedelic-like states) *without* psychedelics for healing purposes. I was lying on the floor with about two hundred other soul seekers who wore plastic mouthpieces (to keep our airwaves open) and eye masks (to stay focused within). I had recently experienced what Stanislav Grof calls a "spiritual emergency," and wanted to validate what my mind, body, heart, soul, emotions, and psyche were going through. My non-drug induced altered realities were fascinating and a little unnerving, so I did what I always do: I dove into my own research and exploration. I found myself on a new journey to experiment and study the different philosophies and teachings of enlightenment and spiritual awakenings.

As I lay down, inhaling and exhaling in a rapid and rhythmic fashion, I got to the point where my whole body was so oxygenated, I felt like I was floating into space. I was breathless, meaning I didn't need to breathe at all as my body remained peacefully still. My fingers and toes tingled with numbness, and I saw wisps of delicate patterns transforming into intricate curvaceous shapes that some describe as the sacred geometry of the Universe. It was so beautiful I began to weep. Weeping, I guessed, was part of the detoxification and healing process that the method promised. Salty tears dampened my eye mask and dripped into the lining of my hair, making it a crunchy hot mess. I felt a soft pressure on my shoulders and feet. I whispered "thank you" to the unsolicited massage angels, because the pressure did not feel like it came from human hands. In fact, no human hands were touching me.

In my mind's eye, I distinctly saw two women who appeared to me as Mother Mary and Mary Magdalene. It was odd for me to see Mother Mary and Mary Magdalene together. I was raised Catholic, so my knowledge of Magdalene at the time was that of a prostitute who used her tears and hair to clean Jesus' feet. Dan Brown's portrayal of Magdalene in his book *The Da Vinci Code* did intrigue me many years ago, but I did not take the time to research further until much later.

Mary sat and held my feet, while Magdalene held my head and whispered the call in my ears. The experience was visceral. When I heard her say, *"Beloved, to be divinely feminine is to be embodied as the Divine. You are the Divine,"* I started to cry even more. I cried because somehow I knew the truth of this, but was too scared to believe it. I cried because I knew that I was supposed to share this wisdom, but had no idea who to share it with. I cried because this mindful awareness event was led by men. I cried because I knew these men didn't truly understand the full embodiment of the feminine; how could they? I cried because I knew that this path meant an old worldview of patriarchal structure must be challenged. I cried because I also thought I might be going crazy.

The reason I share this story is because I know this message was not only for me, but for you. We are being asked to awaken to our subtle senses and listen to what the Universe is trying to teach us and share with us. I can feel your body shiver with a yummy "yes" to this invitation. But if there is still a tinge of doubt left, answer a few questions for me. Have you ever called a psychic or gotten an astrology session, and the readings were eerily accurate? Have you ever been curious about or experienced an altered state (with or without drugs), or had a felt sense in a dream state that was viscerally real? Have you ever contemplated how miraculously you were created from such a teeny weeny sperm and egg, and then grew into your current adult body with no blueprint or directions?

Have you considered that we live on a colorful ball called Earth that is gravitationally held together in a beautiful solar system of planets that float together in a galaxy of a billion trillion stars, and even more planets? Then there are the mysterious black holes and wormholes in this eternally expansive Cosmic blank slate that keeps producing more stars and more planets. This incomprehensible magical Universe is way more unbelievable than a message coming from an archetypal image that invites you to join us in discovering the mysteries of you. There is some serious magic going on around you, and we want you to be a part of it.

{*Lesson: The Divine is calling. Your job is to listen.*}

The Mystery of You

What they forgot to teach us in "traditional" Sunday school is that we are all sacred creatures born through the mysterious lineage of the Goddess.

All creation myths, from ancient wisdom traditions to indigenous earth-based religions, begin with "the void," a place of no-thing, an empty space of infinite possibilities. Then came the "Word," the first vibration of existence, the big bang. It is said that Consciousness had the desire to experience itself, and through this desire and thought (you can insert imaginary starbursts, galactic explosions, cosmic fireworks here) the Universe was born.

The ancient wisdom of the Vedas explains that pure consciousness is a masculine principle of thought and space, represented by the god Shiva. His *desire* to know himself was the spark of the animating force that created the Universe, represented as the goddess Shakti, the feminine principle of All That Is. So in essence, the masculine principle is the *potential* for everything in existence, while the feminine principle *is the everything* in existence. The interplay of both of these opposing forces is required for the perceivable Universe to be a reality. In science, this is called wave-particle duality, or the Universal Law of Polarity. Though polarity, we experience life. We cannot have one without the other, nor are we one without the other. From this understanding, we can begin to experience Oneness.

Trust that your body already knows this wisdom.

Although both energies are necessary for creation on a macro-level and a micro-level, we have managed (in our 3D human form) to value the masculine quality over the feminine quality, which creates imbalances in the world. The mystic and yogi Sadhguru shares that there is no point to the roots of a blossoming tree if there is no blossom. He has said, "If the Feminine does not become alive in you, whether you are a man or a woman, the finer things in life will never happen to you." And since we have landed in this body, on this planet, and have needs and desires, we might as well get back to enjoying the essence and grace of life – the feminine divine.

The mystery of you is that you have the ability to create, gestate, birth, nurture, sustain, enhance, and replenish life. Honoring this feminine nature in you is to honor the planet and life itself. The divine feminine principle *is* everything and *in* everything, so you too are divinely *everything*. This is feminine spiritual consciousness.

More and more women are demanding feminine empowerment, though not every woman knows what that really means for her. Some believe it is smashing the patriarchy, marching on Washington in pussycat beanies, burning our bras, getting on the *Forbes* list of most wealthy female entrepreneurs, wearing t-shirts with rose gold *Goddess Gang* letters printed on them, or striving for sex-positive understanding. I think there is value and truth in all these expressions, but they all are outward expressions of *doing*, rather than *Being*.

Ancient spiritual practices from Buddhism to channeled messages from the higher dimensions, like Abraham Hicks' lessons on the Law of Attraction, all suggest that our outer circumstances reflect our inner thoughts and feelings. So to change the world around us, we must first look inward to change ourselves. To be an empowered feminine, then, is to know the inner workings of the self, to know your superpowers, and to transform any shadow expressions into their higher-octave energy.

What I have come to learn, and what every spiritual teaching offers, is that we have everything we need encoded in our own being. We just need to activate what is called our diamond seed of knowledge. This diamond seed atom holds the whole of you and all that you desire right inside your own body. When it is activated through the integration of all your learning through experience, you will embody your Template of Perfection.

What exactly is the Template of Perfection? My energy teacher describes it as the blueprint of your fullest potential that you, as a sacred soul, have written before you came into existence here on this planet. It is the experience of your highest love, your most potent magic and power, your soul's purpose, and divine truth. From this place of Being, we co-create with the Universe.

Yes, you are that potent and magnetic. This is our amazing destiny.

Now, how are you to find this Template of Perfection? You find it through the process of becoming, or what I call the Arc of Being. It is through the journey of discovering your multi-dimensions of self, and the personas of your inner being that make up the constellation of the current you. When you know and embody the truth that you are this Divine Love, all that you require and desire in this lifetime is spontaneously fulfilled. How you serve with love comes to you naturally because you are *whole*, and therefore Holy, to then receive the abundance and richness and love that exists at this level of being.

One of my spiritual mentors and author of *The Conversations with God* series, Neale Donald Walsch, says, "Don't dismiss the synchronicity of what is happening right now finding its way to your life at just this moment. There are no coincidences in the Universe, only convergences of will, intent, and experience." As I mentioned earlier, we have come together for a reason. Perhaps it is our constellation of such magic that needs to be expressed as reality *now*.

If you are willing to accept this invitation, I'd like to introduce you to the Avatars in the Archetypal Realm who are guiding us. I'd like to help guide your understanding in how they would like to express themselves creatively through you. More and more of us are awakening to the powers of this goddess philosophy, and already feel the influences of her many faces in Isis, Magdalene, Kali, Lakshmi, Kuan Yin, Ishtar, Inanna, and even Wonder Woman. We feel the Great Mother's full expression hidden in the wonder of the curious child, earth fairy, powerful warrioress, femme fatale, demoness, unconditionally loving mother, and wise sorceress as the fragmented parts already in us.

I believe that when we give voice and embodiment to our *many* selves, and interpret the messages from the collective forces that influences us, we gain greater awareness of our inner dialogue. With this awareness, we can exercise more choice and authority over the narration, and finally get to our core essence, void of personality, that is simply an electromagnetic field of infinite possibilities.

{*Lesson: You are the Divine.*}

CHAPTER 2

Love Alchemist

truth

Karma is Watching
The "Zing" of Activation
The Real Dark Night of the Soul
Love Alchemist

Karma Is Watching

"Karma means you are the maker of your life."
—Sadhguru

We are told time and time again that the answers to all our woes begin with unconditional self-love, focusing on the present moment, and meditating. These solutions are a must, and I practice them all the time...*now*. However, some of us can't even think of self-care or self-love, or the power of now, or sit long enough to meditate until we find out what is blocking us from our ability to do these things. This was my experience, at least.

As I mentioned earlier, you are a multidimensional soul on this planet whose birthright it is to express, create, love, and experience all of life. Life does not exist, nor can we experience Her, without polarity, diversity, or contrast. This includes feelings of pain and pleasure, fear and love, separation and connection, shadow and light, uncertainty and certainty, chaos and peace, you get the picture. Not to make things any more complicated, but this multidimensional soul of yours also has many personas or expressions that have agendas, egos, and a contrast of feelings all their own.

Psychoanalyst Carl Jung explains that we come into our lives with a specific master plan that is influenced by the archetypes around us, like our family relationships, memorable events, our culture, and our experiences with nature. These influences are woven into our tapestry of expression in the psyche and in the collective through myths and legends. Jung says, "for reasons of adaptation or personal convenience," a persona arises as a part of the whole. We wear different "masks" for various situations, masks like mother, teacher, executive, author, or spiritual guide. Some of the personas grow from our very own needs to appease others, which give birth to the so-called good girl, the pleaser, the intellectual, and so on.

The basic and universal archetypes that Jung suggests are the victim, the prostitute, the saboteur, and the inner child. We have all embodied the victim archetype through experiences such as bullying, punishment from parents, and arguments with siblings. The action and intensity can vary, like being hit with a belt or getting a "time out." The depth of victim wounding will depend on one's individual sensitivities. Sometimes a harsh word is just as impactful as physical abuse. The victim archetype has an opportunity to turn into the Warrioress. The Warrioress archetype transforms her victim wounds into her power and then helps others.

The prostitute archetype is how we have "sold our souls" in some way to make another person happy, or to follow rules that don't really make sense. The obvious expression is a literal prostitute who sells her body for money. People do this all the time by staying in marriages just for the kids, or out of fear of being alone. The prostitute archetype is expressed through betrayals and lying to oneself and others. Businesses do this all the time by disregarding the earth and the labor force just to make more money. The prostitute has an opportunity to mature into the Lover. The Lover archetype has the capacity to love fully; she will not give any part of herself away to love another person. She loves herself first and foremost, then shares her love from that place.

The saboteur is expressed in the ways we sabotage our opportunities or connections. We become our own worst enemy. The phrase, "I need to get out of my own way" is a saboteur's motto. We've all had moments of doubt that keep us from reaching our fullest potential, or even finishing a project. Self-criticism is what needs to shift in order for the saboteur to become the Magician or Creatrix. The Creatrix archetype is one who co-creates with the Universe. She makes things happen for her, and in the way that is most aligned with her soul's purpose.

The inner child has many facets, depending on the main themes of your childhood. There is the magical child, the eternal child, the wounded child, the abandoned child, and so forth. Often we hold onto one experience that defines our expressions later on. When we grow our inner child up, we become the Sovereign. The Sovereign archetype embodies self-mastery, she is queen of her domain, ruler of her heart, mind, body, and soul. Self-sovereignty is about never having to apologize, explain, or make excuses for oneself.

From each of the basic archetypes, more can evolve. This is why it is advantageous to understand the multifaceted being you have grown into.

Your "blocks" are the abandoned, rejected, disowned, shamed, wounded, repressed, or forgotten personas we also call "shadow selves." They have not yet been able to share their authentic voices, needs, or desires with you, so you aren't aware that they exist, why they exist, or how they are serving you. They unconsciously block our way into our power selves.

From my own experience, and the influences of goddess mystery school teachings and eastern philosophies, the belief that gods and goddesses from the archetypal realm can express through us is a state of consciousness where we can explore beyond this third-dimensional earth plane, and source the higher dimensions for our power and creativity in the world. I have felt the influence of the goddess Lakshmi and Mother Mary all of my life. Thankfully, their good fortune and unconditional love helped me to survive the difficulties I was raised with. As I mentioned, Mary Magdalene has visited me with her divine wisdom, teaching me *hieros gamos*, or sacred union, and the future of partnerships. She whispered to me that it is the divine feminine that will resurrect the divine masculine. I sometimes see Isis, Bastet, and Sekhmet in my dreams. They, and many other divine beings, have influenced my writing, my creativity, and my continued growth as a spiritual being.

Let's add on yet another dimension to this mix. My understanding of how important it is to know the many selves was a long and torturous journey through *many* lifetimes – yes, lifetimes. As I know it, I chose to relive the drama and the chosen karmic lessons in *this* lifetime in order for me to progress to the next set of higher soul lessons. My experience of abuse, betrayal, loneliness, control, fear, worthiness, vilification, and great loss in both my childhood and *this* adult lifetime are reflections of what I didn't learn in past lifetimes. I am going to spare you the details of my lessons here, because I've already written about some of them in my first book, *The Kinky Vanilla Love Project: The Sexy Soulful Journey from Betrayal to Bliss.* Yes, I know it sounds racy. And yes, it does have sex, drugs, and rock and roll in it. But unfortunately, many of us on the path of awakening had to overcome some pretty dramatic experiences before we were raw enough to surrender to the Divine. I learned on Oprah's Super Soul Sunday that the author of *Seat of the Soul*, Gary Zukav, is a former sex addict. The spiritual motivational speaker Gabby Bernstein is a former alcohol and drug addict. The comedian Russell Brand had to overcome his struggles with fame, money, power, sex, and drugs before he found his spiritual path. The many "shames" that happen *to* us are actually things that happen *for* us. I am no exception. Transforming these shadow aspects of our lives is fuel for our superpowers.

My unhealed experiences from *all* lifetimes have helped to create some of my current shadow selves. Now, if you don't believe in past lives, just imagine them as metaphorical experiences animated in your memory by your subconscious to help work out the events that you had to endure. You can also do your own research into the phenomenon of young children recalling their past lives, the wisdom of seers, the near-death experiences that have helped people "see" beyond the veil, or take a guided psychedelic journey if it suits you.

The psychiatrist Brian Weiss, MD is the bestselling author of *Many Lives, Many Masters,* which documents the many past lives of one of his patients during hypnotic regression therapy. The book was given to me after I shared my otherworldly experience of my dear friend's spirit who came to me the night he jumped off the Golden Gate Bridge. The months of him trying to contact me from the other side seemed very scary then; I couldn't comprehend what was going on. I read *Many Lives, Many Masters* in one night and began researching past lives in religious texts, investigated other people's experiences, attended a few Brian Weiss workshops, and eventually tried regression therapy myself. And just to make sure I left no stone unturned, I spoke with mediums, psychics, astrologers, mystics, sages, and scientists on the topic.

Many of my past lives were very exciting. During the prairie days, I was beaten for loving the "forbidden fruit," a native man not of my own race. We were only seventeen, he did not live through the beating, and I died a virgin after a long life of loving him beyond the dimensions of time and space. I was a courtesan to a Mesopotamian king and was wrongly stoned to death for treason. I was one of the early spice traders, estranged by my family for being "too out there." I was hanged for witchcraft. I was a Vestal Virgin who was buried alive because I lost my sacred virginity, even though it was taken by force. I cared for and served food to the 10th Dalai Lama. My baby was taken from me and given to the Sultan's first wife to raise as her own. I was betrothed to a gladiator, walked among the Essenes, and was a Dravidian snake dancer who was stabbed in the back by my lover. I've had many more lives that would make a fascinating miniseries. The details were so vivid, the experience visceral, and they made so much sense to what I was experiencing in this lifetime. This is a way we can learn life lessons, find the clues to our feminine superpowers, experience the goddesses working with us, and discover how to clear out our *karma*.

"Karma" is a Sanskrit word meaning "action." In ancient esoteric and eastern philosophies, it said that our karma is the continuous unfolding of our life over lifetimes, based on our actions and the balanced and contrasting reactions. Here's how it works: all action creates a reaction, then an embodied memory, which then creates a desire that inspires one into more action. This is the Law of Karma.

There are two ways to deal with karma. We can yell in desperation, "fuck you, karma!" and struggle through the injustices and the pains, or we can fuck karma, and enjoy the sensational journey of discovery. I know my words are a bit cheeky here, but my angelic creative guide is a pixie-like provocateur who enjoys being a troublemaker. It's the only way to coax out our shadows, or mine at least. I love her. And since we are sacred soul seekers (in stilettos) who have chosen to accelerate our souls in such a way, we might as well choose to *fuck* karma and delight in the experience while we free ourselves from its control.

Let me digress a moment to explain why I choose to use profanity in a spiritual book that promises to unleash your feminine superpowers and awaken your inner goddess. First of all, it is because I am part human (but mostly stardust). Secondly, my first mentors on the path toward breaking down the façade of my "good girl perfection" walls dropped the F-bomb every few sentences. I found it broke patterns within me, and it felt liberating when I swore along with them. You see, I am from the "other side of the tracks." I wasn't raised with hoity-toity social club etiquette. I have been through the mud and have seen my share of the dark side of life. Still, I had to present myself as a quiet, amicable, stay-way-inside-the-lines, composed, empty shell of a perfect person just to survive. So I trusted the teachers who were bold enough to show their vices, and gritty enough to share their imperfections. We know from the higher realms of consciousness that there is no right or wrong, only judgment of what is. This is one of my imperfections: I swear...a lot. This contradiction within me is also one of my superpowers.

Now back to karma and past lives. "More learning can occur when there are many obstacles, than when there are few or none," says Brian Weiss. "A life with difficult relationships, filled with obstacles and losses, presents the most opportunity for the soul's growth."

The continuous cycle of death and rebirth, called *samsara*, has no distinct beginning or ending. This could feel like an eternal prison if you are working on a few difficult lessons over lifetimes. Our goal is to liberate (*moksha*) the soul from the bondage of karma so we can start co-creating with the Universe. The lives where I was betrayer, castrator, annihilator of men, rageful tempt-ress, and the Devil herself have, to my dismay, come back to haunt me in this lifetime. And so I began my journey into the depths of me, with the dark goddesses at my side: Lilith, Kali, Persephone, Circe, Hecate.

But there is no need to fret. All this gets really good.

{Lesson: Karma may be watching, but we can watch back.}

The "Zing" of Activation

"When you know how to listen,
everybody is the guru."
—Baba Ram Dass

From a divine perspective, everything happens for a reason, and every single event in your life has been priming you for this very moment. My teacher Deepak Chopra, MD calls this synchrodestiny, "a coincidence that contains a purpose and meaning, and has a direction and intention." I love this word because it merges "synchronicities," the concept Carl Jung first introduced as "meaningful coincidences," or seemingly-related events that occur with no causal relationship, with the meaning of "destiny," the idea that events are written in the stars and will eventually happen in the future. "Synchrodestiny" holds the perfect divine essence and balance of co-creation with the Cosmos.

"When you live your life with an appreciation of coincidences and their meanings, you connect with the underlying field of infinite possibilities. This is when the magic begins," says Deepak in his book *The Spontaneous Fulfillment of Desire*. "Synchrodestiny requires gaining access to a place deep within yourself, while at the same time awakening to the intricate dance of coincidences out in the physical world."

I introduce you to this concept now because this is the section where I talk about my spontaneous spiritual awakening, or rather awakenings, which is a process not to be reckoned with. A spiritual awakening can unfold over time. And each time your soul goes through a mini cycle of dying and rebirthing, you get to a clearer vibration of being. Some call this process the ascension of the soul. To me, there is often a first unmistakable moment when you are able to feel the essence of divine bliss in you and in everything *at the same time*. This is Oneness. It doesn't always last that long. Once you know it though, you cannot unknow it. And yes, to awaken spontaneously is "a thing." Watch for it.

In Buddhist practice, these flashes of enlightenment are called *kenshō*, "ken" meaning "seeing or knowing," and "*shō*" meaning "essence." "*Satori*," another term from the Zen tradition, translates as "permanently awakening to your full Buddha nature." A couple of the most famous humans who have reached this state of enlightenment are Jesus Christ and, of course, Siddhartha Gautama, the Buddha himself. I am nowhere near *satori*, but with just a taste of divine oneness and unconditional love, you're hooked. An instant "spirit junkie," as Gabrielle Bernstein calls it. If you listen very closely, you can hear the Divine communicating with you.

A spiritual awakening can come in many different flavors. Eckhart Tolle, the author of *The Power of Now*, experienced deep depression throughout his life until one night he felt he couldn't live with himself any longer. He says that one evening his depression took him to a very dark place and his mind simply collapsed and dissolved. When he woke up the next morning, everything was peaceful. He found peace because there was no self (or many selves, from my perspective). He was left in a state of pure Beingness. And then he spent the better part of two years sitting on a park bench each day experiencing this bliss.

I was riveted by author Anita Moorjani's near-death experience as well. In her book *Dying to Be Me* she describes leaving her body and traveling up into the realms of Love, where she saw that there was no space and time from that vantage point. When she came out of her coma she was miraculously healed from her four-year struggle with cancer. She says that, "Heaven is not a destination, but a state of being."

Some lucky souls are born into their spiritual-ness, such as the 14th Dalai Lama, born Lhamo Dhondup to a farming family in Tibet. The Dalai Lamas are manifestations of realized beings of Buddhahood that have vowed to be reborn again in human form to support humanity. I feel very fortunate to have met the Dalai Lama while on a trip to Dharamshala, India with Deepak Chopra and his family of spiritual explorers. The Dalai Lama and I held hands for about ten minutes. As he spoke to us about happiness, love, and the future of humanity in his joyous way, he would occasionally stick his tongue out at me. Maybe he too remembered our past lives together. Perhaps the shattering experiences in my life were meant to lead me to study *Vedanta*, which led me to studying with Deepak Chopra and to becoming one of his teachers, which led me to India, which led me to the Dalai Lama. This is synchrodestiny.

So many more people are "waking up." Spiritual "knowing" is no longer just for old sages with long white beards and years of lineage behind them, hours of *satsang*, *puja*, prayer, or meditating alone in a cave. As Baba Ram Dass said, "When you know how to listen, everyone is the guru." I hope I can help you listen. We soul seekers in stilettos are now being offered a spiritual runway to strut down. Why shouldn't we all tap into our inner super soul model of divine feminine beingness?

Only now do I feel comfortable sharing my spiritual awakening experience because I now have the support I need. I have attracted my soul family of magical creatures that honor the fluctuations of spiritual growth in this material world. We see no judgment in the messy steps it takes to transform and walk this path of bringing Heaven to Earth and feeling, tasting, hearing, seeing, smelling, and knowing that everything is divine. This path creates changes in your life and your relationships, which can be very scary. Some people will go, and some new people will come into your life. I now see that it is unfair to ask those you love to change with you, or to understand the changes that they will feel in you, or even expect anyone to accept them. That requires them to change as well. Everyone has their own journey, with their own pace of growth, and their own path to take – be it winding, straight, up a mountain, or deep into the muddy earth. In the end, we all get to where we want to go at some point. This is the soul's unique and beautiful journey.

For those of you who have been tickled by the sacredness of all Creation, you can't unknow what you know, you cannot unsee what you've seen, you cannot unfeel what you've felt. So the choice is to either retract back into your small self or expand into your fullest self and hope that your loved ones understand. Retracting into our small selves means that we ignore the pains, the shames, and the struggles we were gifted and simply live as if nothing has happened. Or we fully dive in to experience the dark night of the soul until we find that special golden nugget of hope and healing. As Rumi says, "The wound is the place that light enters you."

My spiritual awakening, and thus tapping into my feminine superpowers, was not such a glamorous or epic tale event, though I do believe the Universe has been trying to wake me up through-out my life. I was simply too stubborn to listen. My childhood was not that easy, and I built an incredible fortress around my body and heart to survive. When I was younger, I saw my father as a rage-a-holic, and my mother as a helpless victim. There was abuse, guns, screaming, blaming, shaming, gambling, lying, cheating, abandonment, and then some. But I have come to the very peaceful and glorious point where I can no longer blame my parents for the pains I witnessed and experienced. My father was the bastard son of an affair. He was fiercely abused, and lived through war, poverty, and death. He was unwanted by his own family. My mother lost her own mother at two years old, and her father had to travel to make ends meet. She went to school in a nunnery until she met my father, her replacement for a loving caretaker. She never got to grow up to be a powerful woman, though it was she who raised us and had two jobs to support her family.

Because of my master skills in creating beautiful yet impenetrable walls, I did experience a devastating betrayal in my marriage that shattered everything around me. I found myself on a rollercoaster ride of healing and self-discovery, not just from the betrayal (that was the easy part), but from all that led up to it, including my past lives. I went through a few dark nights of the soul, which were long periods of deep pain, rage, fear, and grief before feeling even a teeny bit transformed. Over time, the work that I had done led me to understand the importance of forgiveness, gratitude, and love. I know for certain that our pains are our biggest gifts which we choose to experience and learn from. But even then, I still yearned to connect to something "more" that was just beyond me. I didn't really *know* what that "more" was, until I felt the zing of activation.

I had a soul activator. This was not a sexual experience (although he was really cute), it was a platonic chance meeting with an unknowing soul acquaintance contracted by the Cosmos to be in the perfect place at the perfect time. In my astrological charts, my Vertex is in the 5th House in Sagittarius. To some astrologers, this means that I was destined to have a special meeting with a special person for a special reason. By chance, we met for coffee in New York City because we were both there on "business." Our easy one-hour conversation went soul-deep fast, even though we were in the lobby of my hotel. When we hugged goodbye, that was it...*zing!* So simple. The zing of activation came instantly. At first, I thought I was having an early doozy of a hot flash that rose slowly in a wave from my pelvic floor through the top of my head, feeling like liquid golden light, if that makes any sense.

I believe it was our soul-to-soul contact that "woke me up." It could have been the chai I was drinking. Maybe it was the hotel water. Maybe it was from the make-up artist I hired that morning to visually transform my client as she journeyed through her archetypes with me in ritual and photography, and accidentally left some magic dust in my room. But I don't think so. From that *zing* moment on, I would intermittently get intense waves of bliss. Memories of my childhood, the magical parts where I felt really connected to the "world between the worlds," as I called it then, came flooding back to me. I started to sense more, intuit more, and have sudden hits of pure knowing. I felt a greater cosmic vibration around me, and knew that I was part of it. My body felt electric, as if it wanted to connect to something bigger. Yes, I have read many spiritual books, sought out teachers and guides, and have had experiences with loved ones who have passed on trying to contact me in various ways from beyond the veil. But this was different in the way my thoughts and sensations became fully integrated. I felt like I entered a new dimension of what it meant to love and be loved by a force much greater and profound than I have ever known. I wish I had better words for this otherworldly experience.

I'm certain that all of my soul explorations and learnings primed my body for this moment, but it wasn't until that meeting of souls that I actually *felt* an *embodied sense* of true knowing. And then all hell broke loose...

{*Lesson: Soul activation comes in a variety of flavors.*}

The Real Dark Night of the Soul

"When the world pushes you to your knees,
you're in the perfect position to pray."
—Rumi

The dark night of the soul is that defining moment when we are brought to our knees and humbled by the unexpected or unfathomable. The experience changes us. We can choose to rise or be defeated by it. I remember the time my father had a gun to my mother's head, the moment we found out my dad had another family and chose them instead of us, the sting of a belt on my skin. I can still feel my younger self watching my aunt being beaten up by my grandfather and uncles, the sudden death of a dear friend, and the pain and humiliation of infidelity.

Worse for me though, was the vilification and the shaming of my spiritual awakening. Loved ones turned on me and rejected me. All that I believed to be true – the divine feminine, unity consciousness, unconditional love, magic, and my very essence – were stoned, burnt, and hanged to die like the women throughout history accused of witchcraft. I did not understand why I was being thrown into a pit of ravenous hyenas by the very people I trusted the most. My bliss blinded me to the fear of abandonment that people have when they see and experience the subtle changes of growth that they do not yet understand. I was devastated by the loss of some relationships that were very close to my heart, which took me to a very lonely place. But at the end of every tunnel, there is great light. With guidance and understanding, there is always a smoother path to awakening. And as I mentioned, your trials and tribulations are *for* your growth and learning; you will thank them later.

It can take years for your body to settle into her new vibration. The feeling can physically hurt sometimes, and you often feel like you are going a little crazy. At one moment you might be feeling intense love for all of Creation, and the next you might get sick with the loneliness of this knowing. The aftermath is filled with intense emotional highs and lows, and the process is not all that easy or pleasant. This is why I am called to help guide women in the direction of their own self-sovereignty and awakened superpowers. When the *real* dark night of the soul comes to visit, we meet our fears, demons, and shames in order to transform them into light at every single stage of ascension and superpower activation. It is not easy.

I can also see why we humans aren't born with enlightenment. This divine bliss is so ecstatic that our dense three-dimensional bodies cannot handle so much love and light. Our bodies have to adjust to a great deal of heightened energy and emotions first. Bliss is incredible, but if your body is not used to feeling this good, it can be overwhelming. That is what happened to one of my closest friends, and he didn't survive it.

Though people say my late friend was bipolar to explain why he jumped to his death in such a grand way, I think he was having what Stanislav Grof, MD referred to as a "spiritual emergence." A spiritual emergence is what I described earlier: an awakening, usually after evolving beyond the difficulties of life.

Very early that morning, my friend called me to explain his experience of leaving his body the night before, the feelings of bliss, seeing the wholeness of life and how incredible it was. He felt that he had died already and came back into his body at the same exact time and space when he left it. He told me he was not afraid of death because the other side was so beautiful. I'm sure he went through a real dark night of the soul to get to that experience. He sounded sane. He sounded happy. He sounded peaceful. He sounded like he really wanted me to listen. Maybe if he had more support or I had been more aware of how I could have helped him connect to the spiritual dimensions in our lives, in the collective, and on a Universal level, I could have saved him. There may not have been anything that I could have done for him or said to him then, but I do know that he left me a gift and some clues to discover what life and death really mean. On the other side, he helps the souls who have taken their lives make the transition into the light. He still visits from time to time to offer me great wisdom from beyond the veil, especially emphasizing that there is so much to live for and experience on this planet. I am very grateful.

When spiritual change happens suddenly and quickly, the intensity of feelings, thoughts, inner turmoil, and trauma-like experiences in the body can be way too much and way too over-whelming. This causes spiritual crisis or emergency. We do not have much awareness or support to help those who are going through this journey.

This is controversial, but from accounts of near-death expe-riences and my viewpoint that we are all here on this planet to learn, I now look at some forms of mental illness, like depres-sion, addiction, and suicidal ideation in a different way. I see it as the soul's desperate desire to awaken to Spirit and reconnect to Unconditional Love. But instead, our society shames mental illness as something "wrong." Those suffering are given too many drugs to suppress feelings instead of integrating a feeling of connection to something greater, and to a purpose that satisfies their souls. There is such a lack of awareness or training for families that these situations create so much stress, separation, and blame. Labeling people as "crazy" tells those who are suffering to hide, and gives permission for others to turn a blind eye. Some medical professionals feel empowered to immediately prescribe drugs that vary in effectiveness from person to person, without integrating holistic tools to find purpose and meaning in life. I'd like to replace the term "mental illness" with "mental transformation" that differs in scale.

After another one of my "dark night of the soul" experiences, I was on a spiritual mentoring call with Neale Donald Walsch, sharing the various feelings, experiences, and concerns of "awakening." He suggested I read the book *Spiritual Emergency* by Christina and Stanislav Grof. In it they say, "many of the conditions, which are currently diagnosed as psychotic and indiscriminately treated by suppressive medication, are actually difficult stages of a radical personality transformation and of spiritual opening. If they are correctly understood and supported, these psychospiritual crises can result in emotional and psychosomatic healing, remarkable psychological transformation, and consciousness evolution."

So, we aren't crazy, though we might be "woo woo." Our human condition simply makes it hard to get to the exalted and profound experiences that religions and the ancient wisdom traditions describe. Can we transform any of our difficult experiences and become a vortex of loving vibration? Yes, we can.

{Lesson: Hang in there. There is light.}

Love Alchemist

"Just as a wave is a movement of the whole ocean, you are the energy of the Cosmos. Don't underestimate your power."
—Deepak Chopra

Before you entered this Earth plane, you wrote your story from the "world between the worlds" and placed in your blueprint the tools, the magic, the power, the strength, the courage, and everything else you need to successfully journey through your epic life tale. Your Higher Self can reference this blueprint and harmonize to its higher vibration energy whenever you need it. Through this lens, you are the Creatrix of your many lives and your many lifetimes of experiences. We just need to help you remember who you really are.

You might be saying to yourself that there is no way you would have written that particular breakup, that unfulfilling job, the body shame, or the dysfunctional parents. You might even look around and think that there is no way you agreed to the poverty in the streets, the insanity of politics, or the injustices of everyday living. Who would write about the dark night of the soul? I often curse myself for the continued lessons I keep receiving in my most intimate relationships, telling myself I suck as a sacred scribe, and sometimes venting to my unseen guides in the Heavens asking them to back off a bit. We created these devastating contrasts to experience life's opposite. If you have a desire to experience soulful, unconditional, romantic, explosive, nurturing, deeply-intimate

47

love like I do, you have to know what you don't want first. This process requires so much faith and hope in the elegance and grace of the divine that we must learn to let go of fear, and we must trust the perfection of this very present moment.

Even though my reality may not be your reality, I know without a shadow of a doubt that all of our Higher Selves are simply Love, our Templates of Perfection are infused with Love, and our souls are pure Love. In fact, each of us has the power of transformational love encoded within us. We are all love alchemists on a quest to know ourselves through the reflection of our relationships.

Those who have hurt you, unconsciously or consciously, were the first to raise their hand to play this special role that was required in your stories of revelation. These are your bravest and biggest allies. They love you so much that they were willing to be the ones who would inflict the most pain. They are your teachers. And when your consciousness can tap beyond the stories and into the realm of Creation herself, you see how life is really a symphony conducted by the flow of energy, information, and divine intelligence. This feels so much better.

You will begin to transcend time and space and see the infinite potential in each moment. This attracts more of the same type of energy, which allows you to slip into that space where your deepest desires are manifested with ease, your purpose is revealed with grace, your heart is dripping with the nectar of love, and your soul is fulfilled with peace and purpose.

Believing that we have our own unique superpowers gives us access to the superpowers of divine beings such as the goddesses, Arch Angels, Ascended Masters, soul guides and fairy godmothers in the upper realms. Believing makes all this magic work *for* us.

My soul is now demanding that I radiate and reflect Love's Wisdom so that *you* become your own guru, awaken to your Heaven here on Earth, and create and express at your highest truth. I am here purely as your *mirror* of knowing and being.

I am so grateful to share my passion and purpose to amplify love and create beauty on this planet. I do this by sharing a process and understanding that, unquestionably, *we* are incredibly loveable beings that deserve to love and be loved, *epically.* Our wholeness is our holiness, and our holiness allows us to serve and inspire others in meaningful ways. This level of being will open your heart to receive the profound beauty, abundance, wisdom, and love that is running toward you right now.

{Lesson: You are in good hands.}

CHAPTER 3
Rock the Karmic Runway

Rock the Karmic Runway
Ocean of Knowing
The Elementals

Rock the Karmic Runway

"You are a volume in the divine book,
a mirror to the power that created the
Universe. Whatever you want, ask it
of yourself. Whatever you're looking
for can only be found inside of you."
—Rumi

If you haven't guessed already, this book is ultimately about accessing Love, with a capital L, in her highest vibration. We will do this by unleashing your divine feminine superpowers (discovered through the many selves, or facets of our soul), and by meeting some powerful Goddesses, Ascended Masters, Angels, and Spirit Guides who have been waiting for this very moment to meet and support you. This is a vision quest using active imagination techniques to journey into the sacredness of your soul.

In each of the following chapters, I will take you on a guided tour through each of the seven power centers, or chakras, in your body. You will learn about various deity archetypes associated with each chakra, understand the Cosmic Laws related to each power center, and do some practical exercises to help you embody the magic already flowing inside you.

We are the creators of our personal stories, and we will learn from the upper realms why we have written certain experiences and connections into our lives. We will learn how to write our future dreams and live them in the present. My journey, which I will pepper throughout, offered me invaluable insight and wisdom for awakening to our highest potential. I will humbly share who I was, who I am now, and who I am becoming with the hope to inspire you to reveal your truths. I haven't always been connected to or at ease in my body. I haven't always understood the karmic meaning or lessons behind the trials and tribulations, or the betrayals and abuses that I've experienced throughout my life. I have not always felt comfortable, complete, whole, enough, alive, or even spiritual. Although I embrace my many imperfections, and know I will continue to make mistakes and face more challenges, I do feel connected and empowered now because I am tapped into my own channel of divine wisdom. We all have this birthright of miraculous knowing. We all have creativity built into our cells, and the free will to create new circumstances. We are all entitled, as sacred beings, to experience love beyond our wildest dreams.

We will activate your individual archetype in each chapter, and launch their magical force of energy into your love vortex. We will seek out the potentials that inspire you and propel you toward your best self. We will incorporate the many lineages of sacred mystery schools and esoteric knowledge, and learn the Cosmic Laws of Existence. Our goal is to get to your essential self so that you can create what you desire and become the kind of love vortex that attracts and awakens your soul family and maybe eveb your soulmate; directs you to live a life of passion and purpose; and helps you know the wisdom and divineness already in you. This includes transforming our shadow archetypes.

Our journey together will be a soulful exploration of inner and outer beauty, sensuality, and stepping onto your spiritual path... in killer stilettos, if you want. As we unshame and reclaim what is spirituality feminine, your natural and most authentic expression will be revealed. We will welcome the sacred union of the self, where the soul is sensual, the superficial has depth, and the material compliments the spiritual. Here, your feminine power is illuminated at each of your power centers so both its shadow and its most potent light merge and sparkle.

You are a wise and powerful woman who already knows quite a bit about herself. I simply ask that you adopt a beginner's mind, which is both curious and receptive, as we continue on the path together.

In each of the following chapters, we will heal a sacred wound and transform it into its exalted vibration. A sacred wound is a collective pain that we all experience in one way or another. We will honor it as a gift to the earth and for collective healing.

When we call a meeting with the Avatars and your superpowers are revealed, we will identify how each wants to express itself creatively through you. We will give space for acceptance, embodiment, and voice for your revealed selves.

Ultimately, we will get to our core essence, which is void of personality, but is our electromagnetic field of pure potential. From here, you pick and choose when, where, and how much energy to use in any situation that serves your highest vibration of self. All of this will be explained in more detail as we dive deeper into this experience together.

As you continue to read the following chapters, you will be receiving transmissions embedded into my words, and intentions that will activate every cell in your body. A transmission is the sending of energy and wisdom from one being to another. Many ancient traditions throughout the world practiced the transmission of divine wisdom through their unbroken bloodlines from guru to disciple. Today, as I've shared, your soul is awakening;

thus you are already open for direct transmissions from a field of knowledge sourced from the Quantum Realm.

If there is a whisper of skepticism still inside you, please do a little scientific research on your own. Quantum physics proves that solid matter is made up of atoms, which contain subatomic particles called neutrons, electrons, and protons, which are not solid. Atoms are energy. Niels Bohr, a Nobel Prize winning Danish physicist, says, "Everything we call real is made of things that cannot be regarded as real." The theory of entanglement, originally offered by physicist Erwin Schrödinger, suggests that interacting or entangled particles can instantly change in response to each other, even when light years apart. Therefore, energy is everywhere, and it is connected to everything – including you and me.

These transmissions will be expressed and experienced in myth and metaphor. When we open our minds to the language of metaphors, we can travel deeper into ourselves to find the treasures that we seek to give us the happiness, peace, and love we deserve. It is another way the Universe communicates with our subconscious, and how our souls understand what is beyond our understanding. The energy behind metaphors is a collective energy. Rest assured, I will later translate these metaphors into practical processes for you to embody and receive, so you can experience what you have come here to experience. For now, please indulge your subconscious and your soul with the language that she knows best – energy.

The field of knowledge that we have access to is a unique constellation of forces that span the spectrum of vibration from the depths of ancient Atlantis to the heights of the Sirius star system. The wisdom is filtered through my lens and my personal experience with these energies. My own unique expression of this knowledge will communicate with your higher self and your higher guides to activate something new in you.

Remember to keep an open mind and childlike wonder.

In the first experience we will share on our journey together, we awaken to the Earth Empress, float in what I call the *Ocean of Knowing,* and meet the "Elementals." These are nature's avatars, and the five elements of your own personal makeup. We will understand the constellation of your core and activate your Template of Perfection, the master blueprint of your greatest potentiality. We will call on Sirens and Mermaids and other sea creatures to guide us.

We will then land on Eden, where we get rooted and wild at the foot of the Tree of Life to embody her wisdom. Lady Gaia, nature spirits, your magical child, and others await you. Our elemental guide is the Earth herself. We will attend to our rooted power center, where Lilith, Eve, Adam, and the Serpent have something to share with us. We will learn the alchemy of facing your fears with Kali, and what your inner victim (if you have one left) needs before she can turn into your warrioress. Here, we access nurturing love.

Our elemental guide is Water during the second phase of our journey together. Her sensual current will guide us to your hidden magic of creation. We all have the power to create, manifest, and transform. In this watery realm, we may discover an inner sacred prostitute, a Jungian Depth Psychology archetype, who is desperate to stop selling her soul and strives to be elevated to the divine lover. Kali stays with us to activate our inner Shadow Slayer before we float back into the Ocean of Knowing to search for treasures in the dark sea caves. Let us explore what Venus,

Mary Magdalene, and Lalitha have for us as we meet them in the womb space of creation, sensuality, and desire. Here, your radiant beauty awakens and we access intimate love.

Our adventure will then take us into the Pyramid of Light, where we ignite your Holy Warrioress and your electromagnetic super-power. This individual ray of diamond seed light is courageously powerful. Fire is your elemental guide. The goddesses Sekhmet, Athena, and Durga eagerly await to help your inner warrioress engage her Sword of Truth to help access your authentic power and animal magnetism. Here, we access fierce love.

Next we will find ourselves in the heart of Paradise Found, where the Fountain of Youth and your Holy Grail exist in lush abundance. We take refuge here as Lakshmi, Aphrodite, Demeter, Sophia, and the abundance of the heart engulf us. We will have a blossoming ceremony, meet your inner divine masculine con-sort, and embody the Love Trilogy. The heart center is the seat of your soul, where your heart's intelligence takes full control over of your ego to influence your being and doing in the world. Every superpower is filtered through the heart for purification and refinement. Here, we access unconditional love.

We float on air and enter cosmic space, where we will take a deep breath in and then exhale with authentic expression. Your unique creativity is now primed to be displayed out in the world. Air elemental guides Iris, Aura, and Archangel Gabriel stimulate your original voice and the song of your soul. You can boldly express how you communicate love and want to be loved. Here, we access expressive love. The Avatars of Ether help us see beyond the veil. Hecate, Nut, and Saraswati will teach us how to access our third eye of intuitive knowing, to awaken our magic and psychic abilities. Here, we access mindful love.

Finally, we will activate your Almighty Goddess and integrate Shakti, the ultimate goddess known by a thousand different names and faces. She is responsible for creating and animating the cosmos. All the previous deities mentioned are incarnations of Shakti. Shakti energy lives in all the goddesses, and Shakti energy lives in you. She is the universal life force that can be called upon for all our needs. Through this energy, we will integrate each of our power centers and connect the dots of our unique star system, see beyond the veil into truly knowing who we are and why we are here, and be crowned sovereign of our own beings. Here, we access cosmic love.

I do recognize that I have paid more attention to pain and suffering than many spiritually-empowered gurus like to do, but the Divine has gifted me great skills from the shadowy realms, so I must use my superpowers as Shadow Slayer and Shame Smasher (in conjunction with Love Alchemist) to attend to the shadows in order to transform them. I promise I know the light too. As mythologist Joseph Campbell has said, "The black moment is the moment when the real message of transformation is going to come. At the darkest moment comes the light."

Avoiding the shadow side of our being simply postpones its transmutation into something incredibly empowering. Just think of the metamorphosis process of the caterpillar turning into a butterfly. The caterpillar eats the leaf it was born on, and when it reaches its full-grown potential it then creates its own chrysalis. Inside this dark cocoon is where the radical transformation happens. First, it digests itself and disintegrates into a pulp-like consistency. The caterpillar grows imaginary discs, which are potentials for each body part of the butterfly, and these discs use the amorphous goopy liquid to rapidly create the wings and other parts of the body. When the butterfly is fully formed inside the chrysalis, its wings need to be strengthened to break out of the cocoon and take flight. Butterflies in many cultures represent the soul, resurrection, hope, life, change, and beauty. I share this with you because you are a gorgeous butterfly ready to fly.

Are you ready for your metamorphosis, and to become the embodiment of the Divine?

*{Lesson: An open mind and heart is key
to rockin' the karmic runway.}*

Ocean of Knowing

"You are not a drop in the ocean.
You are the entire ocean in a drop."
—Rumi

I hope I've given you enough of a teaser on Consciousness and the Divine so that we can now dip our toes into this Ocean of Knowing. In truth, it is an ocean of *unknowing*, and we must dive into this often uncharted territory to help us know what is unknowable. We go into the depths of our own being because that is where every hidden magnificent gift lies. Fear, doubt, and over-thinking are the only things that stop us from accessing this magic.

The ocean is our primal womb space of safety, nourishment, and creativity. It is the place where all of our information is stored, and where we can float in the amniotic fluids of our beginnings. Here we will find the sea creatures that guide us on this journey together. They are magical and wise, and waiting for your arrival. You are safe here. You can breathe here. You can swim here.

As you dive into the deep, beautiful, and safe ocean, take a long, deep breath in, and then exhale even more slowly. Continue to breathe naturally and easily, focusing on the rhythm of your breath, and let the words on the page sink into your mind's eye. Imagine yourself being able to breathe underwater like a mermaid. Mermaid magic is connected to our senses, emotions, and insight. They can carry spiritual messages into our most raw feelings, touching the depths of our soul and liberating us to the surface where there is more light. Close your eyes for a moment and count to ten, imagining yourself swimming in the deep ocean. You can even try breathing a wave through your torso. Inhale through your nose as you raise your chest and open your heart to the sky, while arching your spine a little. Exhale through your nose by pulling your belly to your spine and rounding your back. Do this a few times in flow to activate your sacral chakra, or *svadhisthana*, where our inner mermaids reside. This type of breath is done in many breathing practices, including Kundalini yoga.

We know so little about the depths of the ocean. Its beauty and color can only be seen through the surface zone where the sun filters through the water. The deeper the ocean gets, the darker and colder it gets, so allow your inner mermaid to help you adjust through this imaginary process. The ocean often represents our subconscious and emotional well-being. I used to have nightmares about tidal waves when I was young. My biggest fear was drowning. Part of this could be from a past life death, but a very real event required me to hold my emotions in for fear of the belt or rage when I was a child. We were not allowed to cry or laugh out loud. We were told that "crying makes you ugly." I believe now that my father was so deeply sad that he would not allow it in others. So the deep ocean was a dark and mysterious place for me, until I went deeper to the source of my anguish and by releasing any blame, I began to feel. When I take clients on this journey, each describe their ocean experience in different ways. Take a moment to think about the deep ocean and what it means to you and journal it.

Through the work of Joseph Campbell, I learned that myths are textured and layered with nuances that tap into the deeper levels of our psyche. They have a mysterious and rich quality to them that evokes our senses toward love, reverence, grace, and beauty. To experience something from the lens of myth and metaphor, we find the multifaceted meaning of the soul.

Now come back into yourself and imagine that all around you is a magical sea kingdom you never knew existed. All the sea creatures you have been fascinated by are swimming near you. There's a bright leafy green sea dragon and seahorses playing together. There are bright yellow fish and iridescent pink crustaceans, a manta ray, and turtles. There is a castle under the sea that you are intrigued by. Swim over to it and enter. What does this castle look like to you? Is it made of crystal or shells or sand or rock? What does the door look like? As you enter, you see yourself in a grand hallway with three entryways. Which one intrigues you most? The one straight ahead, the one to the left, or the one to the right? One of the hallways has a beautiful dim light that calls to you. You go toward it and follow the corridor until you reach another grand opening.

You've found yourself at the opening of an underwater cave. In front of you is an exquisite sea creature. Is it a he or a she? What does it look like? Does it swim fast or slow? Close your eyes now to imagine the details of this exquisite sea being.

This is your emotional chaperone who has been waiting for you to ask for their guidance. My emotional chaperone is a black octopus. The Free Will Law of the Universe requires asking for help when you need it; this applies to any magical kingdom. Guides must be asked before they can help you. On a very practical level, this is good practice for asking what you need and want from your intimate relationships, friends, and family. It is the only way they truly know your needs, it shows vulnerability, and it brings you closer to people. It is also important to distinguish "needy" and true needs. "Needy" has an energy of attachment that feels help-less and requires too much from another person, and eventually turns into resentment. If you are truly in need, you will discover who is in your vibration and who is not. The process of discovering the selves will help with breaking our codependent patterns. The practice of visualization helps you to access your subconscious, and challenges your critical brain to relax. Ask your new sea companion to help you find emotional stability.

When you are ready, your guide swims back with you out of the corridor, into the main room of the castle, and back out into the sea. Look around at all the majestic plants, fish, caves, and maybe even a shipwreck. This is your emotional home. And it is perfect, no matter what it looks like.

You both swim back up to the surface, but before you emerge, you and your guide embrace. They tell you that they are always with you. They hold the keys to your subconscious and will open any door you are willing to enter. They promise you are safe with them. Now take the time to say goodbye and swim up to the surface, where you can catch a glimpse of some sunlight. You feel invigorated by your journey, like you have something exciting you want to accomplish. Write down everything you saw under the sea. Colors, smells, tastes if you had them, and names. Feel the splash of oceanic magic enter the space between each cell of your being.

{*Lesson: The Law of Free Will requires that you ask for help when you need it. Ask!*}

The Elementals

A way to integrate and embody myths, metaphors, and magical knowing is through Ayurvedic wisdom, or the science of life. It is the understanding of how we are intimately connected to the Laws of Nature; the trees being our lungs, the rivers the flow of our circulation, the air our breath that carries the song of our soul out into the world with authentic expression. The earth supports and nourishes our bodies, the sun regulates our temperature, the moon our emotions, the stars our inner guiding light, and so on.

The five great elementals, or *pancha mahabhutas* in Sanskrit, are Earth (*Prithvi*), Water (*Jala*), Fire (*Agni*), Air (*Vayu*), and Ether (*Akash*). These are nature's avatars and the five elements of your own personal constitution that influence how you best experience the material world – in balance or imbalanced. They also affect how we receive divine wisdom, connect to our magic and our ability to create, and how we flow in relationship with others. Each of us has all the elements within us, but some people are more influenced by one element than another.

The Earth element in us is our strength. It is our ability to hold ground and space for ourselves and others. It is how we nurture ourselves and our loved ones. People with predominant Earth qualities are strong-boned, sturdy, have stamina, and are peaceful and supportive. They know how to love unconditionally. With too much Earth in us, we can become sluggish, muddy, and maybe even heavy with depression. Too little, we can become ungrounded. For all of us, with our Earth element in balance, we are calm, steadfast, loving, and we can access Gaia's wisdom. Can you feel if your Earth element is in balance?

The Water element comes in the form of the ocean, lakes, rivers, waterfalls, rain, and tears. Her magic is her sensuality and flow - the emotional current of our inner being. She is heavily influenced by the Moon Goddess. She is the element that impregnates desire, creativity, abundance, and worth. All of us have an equal amount of the Water element in us; we are made up of 80 percent water. The unconscious woman either creates a dam to block the fluidity of her sacred sensuality or allows it to run rabid, depleting herself of its life force. Is your life in flow right now? Does this energy flow through your body as a sensual gift that can be the raging seas, a peaceful river, thunder showers, or the beauty of a dewdrop? Each of us has an abundant fountain of everlasting nectar that helps us move through the world with ease, grace, and magic. What is your Water element like?

The Fire element is an alchemizing force that transforms. She helps us digest our experiences so that we can eliminate, or turn to ashes, what no longer serves us. She helps transmute lower energies into higher energies of pure power. The Sun is the male aspect of such power; however, there is also the sacred light from Sirius, the brightest star in the night sky. She provides us with immense feminine power. The ancient Egyptians associated Sirius with Isis and believed that it was her tears that flooded the Nile river as she mourned the death of her beloved Osiris, represented by Orion. They believed that the first humans came from the star Sirius. So a person who has a healthy Fire essence is intense, radiant, intelligent, energetic, and has a healthy sex drive. Imbalanced, they can be sharp, aggressive, and blame others. What is your inner fire like?

The Air element is the breath of life, or *prana*. The taking in of breath is a holy and divine function. The best and easiest way to get the most *prana* is through the air we breathe, since most of the life-force energy comes to us through our breath. The rest comes from the sun, the food we eat, and nature. It is our inner power. It gives us strength, it animates our life, and is our spiritual essence. Most people access only 25 percent of their breath capacity, which translates into smaller amounts of *prana*. Our thought, our words, and our movement are actions of this life-force energy. People with balanced air quality are changing, agile, energetic, creative, and flexible. Out of balance, there is a lot of anxiety, worry, overwhelm, stress – they can be airheaded. How is your life-force energy?

The most subtle of the elements is Ether, or space. Its significance is that it is void of the other elements and their qualities, yet it is the space from which all the elements are born. Ether is expansive, boundless, and omnipresent. From its emptiness, all elements can fill the space provided by ether. This empty space that holds the vibration of sound is where infinite possibilities exist and where everything begins. Can you empty your mind to tap into the space of boundless potential?

Before we continue to dissect each step in the process of becoming, we will need to take an oath to the elementals. This oath is a transmission directly to sacred Mother Earth and Grandmother Planets. All you have to do now is take a deep breath in, settle into your body, keep an open mind and a receptive heart, activate your wild imagination, and most importantly, surrender to trust. Don't just trust in me, but fully trust that you are ready to know your magic and activate the higher vibration of yourself. Simply allow the flow of ease and grace and epic love to enter your heart now. Say the following out loud:

I am ready to dive into the ocean of my inner being and find the guidance that I need to lead me toward Lady Gaia, Mother Earth, the Earth Empress. She is the original material mother who holds and loves every single sentient being, "good or evil," no matter what – including me. She is the mountains and the structures that hold me steady, she nurtures me unconditionally, she provides for me without hesitation or lack.

I am open to the watery flow of creativity and sensuality through me. My womb space is ready for my soul's deepest desire to be manifested, and I am ready to elevate all my energies to an even higher vibration of love. I welcome the Venus within me to rise up from the foamy seas into my heart.

I allow my unique rays of fiery light to radiate through my body and into the world around me, to inspire and empower others in my own way. I am grateful for the transformational goddesses to infuse me with their powers to help me activate my own.

I inhale the breath of life to enliven my being and connect me with everything on this planet. I welcome the wisdom of the air entities to permeate every cell in my body. I exhale only love out into the world.

I pause in the space of no-thing, allowing the ether to open my third eye to the worlds beyond my world and dimensions beyond my wildest imaginations. I trust this cosmic space that holds my highest potential of Being.

Just sit with that for a moment, and allow the words to enter your skin, through your muscles, and into your bloodstream. Repeat it any time you want.

Love Avatar

CHAPTER 4
Rooted & Wild Feminine

Earth Empress

Welcome to the New Eden

Template of Eve &
the Return of Lilith

I Kissed the Devil and I Liked it.

Rooted & Wild Feminine

Earth Empress

Until we get to the most essential part of ourselves, we should continue to ask this very important question: *Who am I?* How convinced are you that the most exquisite creature on this planet is you? Do you believe you are capable of lighting up the world, creating your destiny, and loving in unimaginable ways? Since change is the only thing that is constant in this visible universe, and evolution a must, *Who am I?* is a worthy question for the presentational self. When you ask yourself this question every night before you go to bed, you will allow your subconscious to tap into your eternal self to help answer the question as you sleep. The integration of your presentational self and your eternal self helps you *be* on this planet as you initially intended.

Speaking of planets, here we are on Mother Earth, the most beautiful planet in our solar system. It's a miracle to think about how many planets there are in our Milky Way galaxy (more than 100 billion!), and just as many stars. According to science, in order to support life on any planet, there must be water and the planet must sit in perfect placement within its solar system so it doesn't fry up or freeze. Although it is obvious that I am among those who believe there *must* be other life forms in this ginormous universe, scientists have not yet detected the unmistakable presence of life form on any other planet outside Earth. This too is miraculous, and begs the question, who am I on this planet?

Many occult beliefs share that Earth is a school where our souls come to learn and grow. You've probably heard the phrase, "we are not bodies with a soul, we are souls in a body." Our souls are housed in this temple made of flesh and bones. Each of us had a desire and choice to "separate" from Source, the core energy that *is* existence, to become the soul that animates our bodies. Each of us has an over-soul that vibrates at a higher level and guides us as we experience the contrasts here on this dense material plane. You chose to be born through your parents, in your body, through your star constellation, and to experience the lessons that would allow for your soul's ascension. Mother Earth is that school for everyone's soul journey.

Ancient philosophies from around the globe hold Mother Earth in reverence for supporting our existence. From the biblical text Genesis 2:7, "God formed man of dust from the ground and breathed into his nostrils the breath of life, and the man became a living creature."

We are not only symbiotically connected to nature, we are part of nature and nature is part of us. Our first mother as humans *is* Mother Earth. As helium and hydrogen make up her stars in the sky, they are also in atoms that make up our bodies. She gives us abundant air to breathe, and her sacred plants offer us the necessary oxygen to live, while we give them the carbon dioxide to thrive. Her rivers that nourish the earth to grow the foods that feed us are like the veins that carry our nutrient-rich blood to circulate through and nourish the body. Mountains are like our bones, giving us structure and strength and majesty. Like us, Mother Earth expresses herself as lighting, thunder, a soft breeze, an earthquake, stillness, and beauty. You are all of these things. Reverence for and communing with nature awakens your primal magic, and primal magic is your inherent impulse for survival.

Our primal magic lives here in the root chakra, or power center at the base of our spine, where our instinct for survival lives. These instincts are fight, flight, freeze, and fornicate. At this level of consciousness, our thoughts, feelings, actions, and reactions have to do with the desire to survive and the traumas associated with this desire. Fear and shame also live in this chakra. This primitive response is grounded in the sympathetic nervous system found in our primal brains, serving to protect our bodies. When triggered, our blood pressure rises, our heart beats faster, we experience rapid breathing, our adrenaline increases, and our immune system is repressed. Although we no longer live in fear of being eaten alive by the saber-toothed tiger, our stress triggers are still trapped in the reptilian brain and can show up in a more genteel version, such as defensiveness or criticism. Our responses to life's situations and relationships are reactive at this level of consciousness.

Activating the root chakra allows us to feel safe, worthy, and abundant in the world. In order for us to experience the next level of our divineness, we must transmute the lower survival instincts of fight, flight, freeze, and fornicate into their higher octave – fearlessness, freedom, flow, and fulfillment.

Our primal magic is worthiness and trust. We must trust that we are safe and that the earth is abundant, and we must know that we are worthy enough to receive her gifts. The way we feel safe and secure in this world is by staying fiercely rooted to Mother Earth's core to access her great wisdom and to take the steps to awaken the sacred serpent that lay at the foot of the Tree of Life, which we will get to later in this chapter.

My personal understanding of the wisdom of the Goddess and Earth Consciousness came to me during a shamanic journey. I actually *heard* Lady Gaia scolding me, in the most nurturing and loving way, for not having reverence for the earth. Many psychic mediums will say they either *hear* or *see* messages that they must interpret. Others *feel* their knowing. All of us have this ability, and tuning into earth's energy can help awaken these subtle senses.

Through my mind's eye, I argued with the Mother Goddess about this. I absolutely cared about the preservation of our forests and cleaning up the oceans. I always try my best to recycle, reuse, reduce, and renew. But she knew that I was more interested in what was beyond the stars; I never thought about the magic on *this* planet. As she scolded me, I felt held by her without judgment. She was right. Although I was earth conscious, I was not Earth Conscious. My head was always in the clouds, I never felt grounded or belonging to this earth. My 23andMe DNA test shows that I have a small percentage of unknown DNA, which convinced me that my ancestry was definitively star born, from Sirius to be exact, as confirmed by an Akashic Records reading. I have been guided toward the stars to quell the feeling of being an outsider on this planet, so I wanted that reading to be true. What I really needed was to focus on the glorious planet that I was living on.

Mother Earth is the ultimate nurturer and provider. She teaches us the interconnectedness of every living thing, and the beauty and abundance of being. Every flower is different, yet each blossoming is beautiful. Earth Mother does not judge, but holds and accepts the diversity of everything and everyone that takes from her. All species and organisms, no matter what kingdom, breed, race, religion, ideology, personality type, or temperament are embraced by her. She does not fight the cycles of the seasons, she surrenders to the rhythm of death and rebirth.

Lady Gaia came to me like a teenage girlfriend and asked if I wanted to visit the Tree of Life, a widely known archetype from many religions and esoteric philosophies that represents the connection to all things in creation. Lady Gaia took my hand and guided me to this most magnificent tree that was illuminating with iridescent light. To me, it looked like it was surrounded by thousands and thousands of fireflies or fairies, little messengers that could converse with the Heavenly creatures and earth entities. Lady Gaia then asked if I wanted to *feel* what the Tree of Life felt like. And of course I did. She took me into the most sensual and loving experience, where I effortlessly flowed with the felt sense and understanding that all of nature is connected, we are all connected, the whole universe is connected to everything. I felt how much love there was on this planet, and how eager she was to help us heal our wounds so we could all feel held and nourished. I felt united, in flow, ethereal, important, unimportant, guided, sensual, powerful, and true.

Belonging, Mother Earth said, is our birthright. Those of us who feel lonely at times forget that the earth is always here to provide for us. Earth energy is quite powerful, beautiful, regenerative, and very wise. Just imagine what kind of power comes from the gravitational pull of her center. The earth formations above the sea and under the sea are exquisite. There is so much diversity and abundance in plant life and animal life on this planet. The plants, animals, insects, fungi, and everything in between should be considered sacred, too. When humans leave the earth alone, she regenerates.

Lady Gaia is the Earth Empress who gives us life, nurtures life, and sustains life from the planet's natural resources. She transforms for us each season. In the winter, she rests and rejuvenates. In the springtime she comes forth as the child of awe, wonder, and innocence, full of the newness of life and the bearer of hope. You might feel her as a breath of fresh air or light bubbling from your skin. During the summer she is like the woodland nymphs and sprites, making sure that everyone's desires are blossoming and blooming. She feels like radiance here. In the fall, she might take on an animal-like form, allowing her to luxuriate in the changing of the season and preparing for the winter. You know you are already guided by Lady Gaia if you have a keen interest in being a steward of the earth. She tells me that everyone can embody her gifts.

Now that you are more comfortable with the understanding that you can access the source of pure potential and manifestation on this planet and beyond it, and that you have the most incredible earth guide to take you to the center of the planet and to your most rooted self, we can now travel to the place where we *very first lived*.

{*Lesson: Your birthright is belonging and worthiness.*
Claim your space on this planet.}

Welcome to the New Eden

"You know what the issue is with this world? Everyone wants a magical solution to their problem, and everyone refuses to believe in magic."
—Once Upon a Time

I want to take you to Eden first. It is that paradise in your own body where pleasure, abundance, innocence, purity, and sacredness exist. We will enter the temple of Eve and witness the return of Lilith later, two very controversial women from a patriarchal point of view. First, I want you to remember your harmless and untamed personality *before* any conditioning or blocks held you back, *before* the first offense on your body or soul when you were judged, shamed, or taken advantage of, *before* you had to follow rules that censored your truth. *Your* Eden is the place of pure loving, a place to freely and curiously allow your inner child to flourish. She believes in magic, she is present, she knows exactly what she wants, her dreams are gigantic and far-fetched, and she truly believes they will all come true. She expresses her emotions without hesitation, before cleansing them from her body without shame. She believes that butterflies and rainbows make everything that much better. Here, in this garden of your soul, we activate the magical mind.

The magical mind is the mind that has no ego. She is in service to the heart and soul. The magical mind is the knowing mind activated in the pineal gland, which is a tiny endocrine gland in the center of our brain that regulates melatonin. Some people, mostly spiritual gurus and psychedelic experimenters, call it the third eye for its consciousness-expanding experiences and potent transcendental visions. It can be stimulated through active imagination, breathwork, meditation, or psychedelic medicines. I believe that when we are very young, our "heavenly eye," as the Taoist called it, is already opened and we are much more tapped into the world between the worlds. As we age, our pineal glands slowly turn off. According to Wikipedia, an estimated 40 percent of Americans get calcification of the pineal gland before they are seventeen years old due to the heavy fluoride in our water; no wonder we don't believe in magic anymore. When we tap into the magical mind again, we give ourselves permission to see beauty in everything. We see that the exquisiteness of nature is a reflection of the beauty within us. This process of envisioning, feeling, and integrating the experience in the body in order to take advantage of our brain's neuroplasticity is what I call Magical Mind Shaping.

Let's allow Lady Gaia to take us on a journey through the Tree of Life as I did, to your root center, where the Serpent of Kundalini Energy lies dormant in the base of your spine. "Kundalini" is a Sanskrit word meaning "coiled snake." It is mentioned in the early Vedic sacred texts known as the Upanishads, which are over 6,000 years old (c. 1,000 BC–500 BC). Kundalini was a secret practice for thousands of years, only shared with those who were deemed worthy of the knowledge. Kundalini is an energy of sacred creation and life-force that, when activated, connects us directly to the Divine. This energy, when awakened, spirals through each chakra to alchemize into their higher frequencies. Our fears, shadows, and karmic lessons transform into the light of truth and power. When Kundalini arises, we experience a spiritual awakening in the body.

In this next transmission, we will meet your earth guardians and your wondrous, magical child and learn what they have to teach you at this moment. Take a deep breath in and exhale, get into a comfortable position, and take a moment to close your eyes and visualize the ocean before you continue reading.

Imagine yourself floating again into the ocean full of possibilities, until you see before you the shores of the most exquisite land, you see the lushness of the sacred plants, and you feel the sand between your bare toes. The temperature is perfect for your skin. You feel very comfortable here. The sun is shining. There is a pathway through the lush gardens and you make your way through the plants, smell the scent of the blooming flowers, the bark, maybe even the fresh scent of morning dew. You notice the beautiful flying iridescent creatures in a spectrum of colors, and their song sounds like the whispers of a bumblebee. You can hear the wind tickling the leaves and the crunching of earth beneath your feet. When you lick your lips you can taste the salt of the sea, making your mouth thirsty for water.

Continue walking on your path until you get to a clearing. In front of you is a magnificent tree, illuminating with iridescent sparks. It is magnificent. There is a passageway into the tree. You go to it and step in. It is hollow and dark. There are stairs in the hollow tree and you decide to take the ten slow steps down through its center until you reach the bottom. At the foundation of the earth, you make your way forward to see a hint of light in front of you, so you follow the light until it gets brighter and brighter and brighter. There is a clearing that opens to an emerald forest full of trees, birds, rainbows, waterfalls, and mountains. It is the world between the worlds. You see an animal cross your path. Stop to think about which wild animal you saw or are most intrigued by.

There is no right or wrong answer, but oftentimes animals that you are captivated with are representations of primal energies within you, wanting to be expressed. If you don't see one, that is appropriate too, as each person is unique. Many of us who live in unity consciousness have either experienced these primal energies first hand, while others blend the many belief systems that work with animal energy because the essence of this power is universal. Ancient cultures of the Philippines believed that everything had an *anito* spirit, including the rocks, the plants and the animals. In Hinduism, it is said that the creator god, Brahma, hid secret spiritual gifts in animals. The use of totem animals is associated with Indigenous Native American practices. I'm splitting hairs here, but for our purposes, a guide animal is one (or many) that has come to support you, give you a message, or is one you can call on for its unique energy to help you in a situation. Guide animals can stay with you for as long as you need, or for just a moment. Your soul animal reflects your emotional essence and the subconscious parts of you that others might not see. Your power animal is the animal that you would be if you weren't human. I would be a black panther. For me, a black panther is mysterious and provocative, she is equally elegant and fierce, she exudes raw dark power, yet is sensually feline. I use all her qualities in my work and in my art. But when I do this exercise, I often see a male lion protecting me and guiding my path on earth. I have the soul of an octopus. We will revisit this again, but please be flexible and don't get too attached by these definitions, because we are all really shapeshifters flowing through various animating forces as we continue to evolve and grow. Use these primal energies to guide, inspire, and ignite you, not define you.

Think about the qualities and gifts of the animal that you chose (or that chose you), and why you are intrigued by this animal, the way it walks or flies or slithers; its color and sound significance; how it spends its day or night. You do not have to look up animal meanings to get it right. The answers are already inside you. Since we are training for our own self-sovereignty, and activating our unique superpowers, your answer is the right answer – trust it. This will give you some clues to your innate talents that are most foundational to you.

Your new animal guide takes you through the lush jungle. As you meander behind this animal, you feel safe as it transports you even deeper into the core of the earth, and the path begins to soften until you come to pools of clear water amongst many grass knolls. The water is so clear that you can see your reflection in it. There is one very special pool; it is the pool of innocence, where it is said that if you drink from it, you will go back in time and remember the time of magic and purity when you were still connected to the magic of the earth in your youth.

You can feel the pull of those waters and when you come to it, you kneel down and take a drink. When you are fulfilled, you raise your head to see your own reflection as the ripples settle into glass-like stillness. You are fresh with wonder, fascination, and joy. There are no stress lines on your face, no aches in your body, no worry about what others think. As this wondrous magical childlike being, you understand that there are no conditions here, no rules. Only love and the canvas to create and become anything you would like to become. Your guide animal asks what it is that you came to create and become in this world. What do you say to your guide? Take a moment to write down your dreams and hopes for this world, the ones that are beyond your wildest imagination.

I want to remind you that hand-writing your thoughts on paper activates the right side of your brain, which transports you into a trance of creative thinking. Some people can channel the messages from divine source through freewriting, which is asking a question and simply writing the answer without thinking about it. This is what author and spiritual mentor Neale Donald Walsch did to write his book series, *Conversations with God*. This is what I am asking you to do when I have you pause to journal. I'm asking you to free associate in order to awaken your channeling prowess.

Now back to the New Eden...

You and your sacred animal guide come across two women standing at the base of a beautiful fruit-filled tree. They offer you a piece of the fruit, and without question, you eat it with delight. The nectar runs down your face and you sip its juice in rapture. Every cell in your body begins to wake up. It is the juice of truth.

You notice there is a serpent at the base of the tree. You are unafraid, and your animal guide relaxes beside you. The snake ever-so-slowly slithers up to you and uses its long tongue to taste your skin before she slides up the inside of your left leg. This sensation feels oddly sensual to you. Before you know it, this serpent has entered your body and coils itself up to rest in your pelvic floor at the base of your spine. You can still feel its continuous breath and pulse.

The two women smile at you, knowing. You have many questions for the two women in this magic place of manifestation, potential, and creation. They remind you of the reason why you entered this glorious earth and what you came here to learn and accomplish. They support you as you create your life's journey from beginning to end, the people you want to meet, the experiences you want to have, and why. You create your loves, your losses, and your greatest accomplishments. You are so thrilled by the incredible story you've created that you add in more gifts and challenges that will become the refinements of your superpowers. They have you pause at the moment when you realize how powerful and creative you are. They ask you to stand erect while rooted to the earth, heart lifted and open to the sky. The top of your head is balanced as if you wore a jeweled crown worthy of the Earth Empress that you are.

Get out your journal, put some classical music on, and do a freewriting exercise about this journey into the center of the earth – your Eden. Write your story from beginning to end. Do this with a timer set to three minutes. Alex Faickney Osborn, co-founder of the advertising agency BBDO and author of the creative technique called *brainstorming* says, "It is easier to tone down a wild idea than to come up with a new one." And, "Each of us has an Aladdin's Lamp which psychologists call creative imagination." Timed writing helps us shut down our critical mind that makes us want to edit every word and phrase to be as fantastical as J.K. Rowling and as magically poetic as Gabriel García Márquez. It's time to write now!

{*Lesson: Magical Mind Shaping is your roadmap
for your inner journey.*}

The Template of Eve and The Return of Lilith

> "Eve tasted the apple in the Garden of Eden in
> order to slake that intense thirst for knowledge
> that the simple pleasure of picking flowers and
> taking them to Adam could not satisfy."
> —Elizabeth Cady Stanton

Many of us who embrace our feminine essence are still unconsciously caged by the stories of an Eden full of betrayal, temptation, and banishment. I feel compelled to repeat this until every woman reclaims her birthright to not only taste the truth about her awakened knowledge, but also to understand the truth that she already *is* knowledge and life embodied. Women are haunted by original sin for just being born women. As the story goes, the feminine ideal represented by Eve was tempted by the seductive serpent to taste the fruit of knowledge. Men, represented by Adam, were tempted by the curious Eve in all of us to know the unknowable. So they took a bite, and descended into the hells of duality, contrast, separation from spirit, shame, and the other deadly sins. From that first bite, women have been punished for the creation of shame, the fall of man, and all other sins. We have been made to feel guilty by the epigenetics of this story ever since.

But there is so much more to this tale that has been omitted from its original texts to serve a dominating culture that vilifies the soul essence of human existence. Missing from this origin story are any references to the creative, powerful life-force energy that creates, gestates, and births life – the very power of woman.

What if Eve was the awakener of mankind, and the snake was life-force energy? The serpent, in many ancient wisdom traditions, is the power, sensuality, sexuality, and vital creative force within each of us. The fruit represents that our awakened senses are important to an embodied consciousness, and reminds us that we are spirits in a goddess-given body, not bodies to be shamed. To stifle and shame this animating life-force energy innate in our body, the serpent power, is to turn off the very essence of light, love, and life.

There is something very wrong with the blaming of the feminine for the fall of mankind. As you recall, Consciousness was curious to know itself. This desire sparked everything into existence. Eve's temptation "to know" is simply a brilliant expression of her divine intention to experience herself in her wholeness.

Eve represents everything about a woman a man should guard against. Because of this outdated image, all women are burdened by Eve's reputation as disobedient, guileless, weak-willed, prone to temptation and evil, disloyal, untrustworthy, deceitful, seductive, and motivated purely by self-interest. Essentially we are to be blamed for everything. Feel within. Are you still caged in domesticity, puritanical ideals, and the shaming of your truth?

The story of Adam's first wife, the powerful and equal Lilith, is often untold. She was cast out of Eden for refusing to be dominated by Adam and lie beneath him in submission. When Adam became lonely (and probably sex-starved), he asked God to bring Lilith back to him. Lilith, with her newfound freedom, had birthed hundreds of children on her own. When she refused to return to an unequal existence with Adam, her babies were slaughtered by punishing angels, an experience that, rightfully so, erupted her vengeful rage. It is my interpretation that this story was to scare women into being submissive to their husbands or be subject to the symbolic butchering of their children, a mother's deepest fear. Some versions of Lilith claim that she is the serpent, a portrayal of a woman betraying another woman. This imagery also causes the dismantling of the sacred bond of sisterhood, which weakens the power of woman once again.

In both interpretations, Lilith is punished for her insubordination and lustful, rageful demonic expressions. Her power got demoted to the reason why men have affairs and women seek revenge. It seems convenient to create a story about women who are to blame for sexual shame, and to vilify them because they demand equality. Isn't this yet another example of how low-level, unconscious men fear the sexual power of women?

Let's sprinkle a little feminine stardust truth onto this Lilith tale. As her sovereign self, fully actualized and whole, Lilith granted Adam a moment in cosmic time to express his shadow side of insecurity and insignificance in the world. Lilith, with her generosity, wanted Adam to feel his dominance in the world, so she split off part of herself to become Eve. She did this to offer Adam a more demure and accommodating aspect of herself (as Eve) to keep him company on his sojourn for world dominance, and then guide him back home to self-knowledge through the experience of the body. Sadly, Lilith had no idea what kind of unconscious animal he would become. Both feminine archetypes – the demure Eve, devoted to Adam, who is too weak not to give in to temptations, and the independent and rebellious Lilith, who can wreak havoc on any man – warn the masculine not to trust women, and women not to trust themselves or each other.

As you may have guessed, the two women in *your* Eden are Eve and Lilith, the archetypes of the two different types of women that exist in the minds of every (perhaps emasculated) man. They have been trapped in the garden of good and evil, the disgraced Eden, for too long now. In our shame and humility, we departed from the original Eden because of the vilification of sex and temptation. It is only by transforming sex into its exalted form of life-force energy and vibration of sacred union, while simultaneously transforming our "temptations" into divine intention that we shall reclaim our Eden. Once we return to Eden as the embodiment of the Divine Feminine, free of shame for our nakedness, our sexuality, and our decision to honor and know the truth about ourselves, we must also ask for the return of Lilith within each of us. *That* will be powerful.

You do have a superpower that will help free both Lilith and Eve from the "garden of good and evil" Eden, so that you can help restore Eden into a Paradise Found. When your inner Eve and Lilith are free from fear, shame, and exile you will begin to awaken the serpent within, you will be able to commune with the Earth Goddess, and you will begin to recreate the foundation of your own existence. Let's commit to a new paradigm for both Eve and Lilith in Eden – Eve as a representation of the process of awakening humanity to their higher truth, and Lilith as the sexually equal feminine archetype who refuses to be dominated by man. The merging of these two aspects of woman is when your senses heighten, you feel the electromagnetic pulse of your own power, you understand the mirror of your relationships, and you just "know."

{*Lesson: Through the divine merging of Lilith and Eve
within you, liberation follows.*}

I Kissed the Devil and I Liked It

The power of resurrecting the Lilith archetype is even written in the stars. For the astrology devotees among us, did you know that where your Black Moon Lilith falls in your astrological charts can tell you a little bit more about your fears? We are so excellent at hiding our shadows that sometimes we hide them from ourselves. Anything that triggers disgust or judgment in us is a very potent hint of the deep pains we would like to avoid. Our vulnerabilities and the raw and impulsive instincts that are buried deep in our very essence are represented by where this point in the sky lands among the constellations. Surrendering to our most honest longings and truths that we keep hidden in the deepest parts of our soul is what the Black Moon Lilith is asking of us. What is your heart yearning for? What does your soul crave? What is your body thirsty for? What are your deepest fears?

Fear. We have all experienced it. You've heard that "fear is the root of all evil," but we aren't here on this planet to experience fear. We are here to love and create. Transforming our fears is necessary to feel truly safe on this planet. Lady Gaia guided you to your root center at the Tree of Life and introduced you to the Serpent of Kundalini Energy that lies dormant in the base of your spine. As mentioned, this serpent energy, when awakened, spirals through each chakra to alchemize them to their higher frequencies. At the rooted power center, our fears, shadows, and karmic lessons can transform into the light of grounded power, nurturing love, the seat of womanhood.

Love Avatar

During my own experience through the heart of the earth with Lady Gaia, she took me to all the dark places in my psyche and my soul. I had long accepted my shadows, so the experience was not as scary as one might think a meeting with the demons might be. Mother Earth showed me how good I am with navigating the dark side. She told me to give the earth all my pains, shames, fears, toxins, and diseases so the lower creatures like maggots, mites, cockroaches, and other creepy crawlies could evolve as well. The earth wants all of the things that do not serve us emotionally or physically. Other people do not need our negative emotions, although your loved ones can learn how to support you as you send all negative energy to the earth. I met dragons, cooked in the transformational fire of the Phoenix, and met the Devil. I learned the spiritual steps to overcome fear.

As my journey into the descent of Hell began, I felt myself slowly walking down a long dark cave-like corridor. I was not at all resistant, as I already anticipated that I was going to see yet another shadow aspect of myself. As I walked even further into the center of this ominous space, I could feel an oppressive and chilling presence, and I knew. I knew that I was going to the darkest place, the seventh circle of Hell where the Devil himself dwells with the violent souls, too lost to see the destructive world that they had created. I had an option to succumb to fear and allow the victim in me take over, as I had done many times before in my life, or walk toward the fear – yes, still a little afraid. I chose to travel forward.

As I continued on, I saw the dominating presence of evil itself, huge, menacing, without any light. This is when I had to pull from my center all the power and bravery within me. I took in a deep breath of courage that allowed my spine to stand erect and tall.

I felt my energy, a luminescent golden light, go deep into the earth and far up into the heavens. Without another thought, I walked straight toward the Devil. Our eyes locked. The Devil pretends nothing. He is fear itself. He did not move, but allowed me to come to him. With focus and intention, I stepped forward. For a brief moment, I assessed how I would destroy this despicable thing in front of me and realized that I would have to turn into a demoness in order to match the magnitude of this amount of gloom. So I became the She Devil. I have to say, it felt quite powerful, like nothing I've ever experienced. But I believed that it would be a fair fight if I took on the Devil as the Devil. I advanced forward.

I found it puzzling why the Devil did not attack me or make a move, though his company was terrifying. I wondered what kind of war tactic he had up his shadowy sleeve. Face to face with the Devil, I understood that it was my choice to fight this thing or be consumed by it. I looked into his menacing eyes, aware that my very first touch would ignite the weapons of sinful destruction. Oddly I found that time stopped, and for a millisecond it offered me the utmost clarity. With calmness, security in my body, and inner knowing, I went for it.

As a wave of pure light engulfed me, I leaned in and kissed the Devil on the lips. In that millisecond of time, I felt the love of all beings, including the demons. And I knew. I knew that fear thrives on fear, and the only thing that can conquer fear is love. In fact, fear is simply the shadow side of love. As I kissed the Devil with all the love in my heart, we merged like lovers in divine ecstasy. In an instant, our bodies were engulfed in flames that became the blaze that fueled my transformation. I cooked in this fire of transformation until I could feel all the darkness melt away and wings emerge. With renewed light in my heart, I regenerated into a new form and took flight as the Phoenix who then turned into an eagle, another guide animal to provide me with foresight as I journeyed on this planet.

Transforming your fears first begins with a choice to walk toward and face your fears. Walking toward your shadow side is courageous. Courage requires a bit of hope, and hope is always laced with love. The choice for me was to lead with fear or be led by love. I chose love. Our fears are nothing without the energy they need to multiply. So walking toward or being aware of your fears stops their viral spreading to all relationships and experiences in your life. Facing your fears head-on is your commitment to transformation.

The second thing to do is to become your fear, with conscious awareness and love. To become your fear simply means to understand it completely and with compassion. It is owning the shadow side of your being, and understanding that the outside world reflects what is going on inside. We attract the people and experiences at the level of consciousness we participate in. Since you are the Creatrix of your life, when you live by fear, you will attract more things that offer you the validation of your fear. If you choose to be led by love, more loving experiences and people will start coming into your life.

The third aspect to resolving fear is to love it. Love that part of you that has been victimized or taken advantage of. Love that part of you that judges, criticizes, and blames. This is why we become our fears first; otherwise, we will never know that fear is within us. We cannot see in another what is not in us. Adding love diffuses the poison and you will begin to forgive yourself. Practice gratitude for the people who gave you the opportunity to find the courage and the opportunity to conquer the unconquerable.

{*Take a moment to do an exercise with me. On one page of your journal, reflect on the top three people in your awareness that you despise. Write their names down and all the qualities you dislike about them. Then pick three people you admire most in the world, and write down all the qualities that you admire about them. Pause from reading to do this exercise.*}

{*Lesson: Transformation:*
1) walk toward 2) face 3) become 4) love your fears.}

Rooted and Wild Feminine

"The wild woman has a deep love of nature,
a love for the ancient mother. Though
possibly misunderstood, it has always been
in her. When she goes into the wilderness
a part of her soul is going home."
—Shikoba

Oftentimes, it takes a rupture in our lives to gift us the wakeup call to step on the path of self-discovery. Some of us are so stubborn that we need a few bricks in the face to wake us up, or we have to meet the Devil himself. It doesn't have to be this way, thank Goddess.

Take a look at the list of "bad" and "good" qualities you just wrote down. To make the most of this exercise, please don't read further until you've written yours down. Then choose the three negative qualities that bug you the most, and choose the three that you admire the most. Write them on another piece of paper. Now get rooted into the earth and tap your heart with your fingers to get out of your critical mind for this.

The three "bad" qualities are the ones you still have in you that you are hiding from or fear the most. The three "good" aspects are the characteristics you are striving for the most. Every time I do this exercise with my sacred rebel sisters, they get mad at me for just a little bit. But stay with me. The first time I did this exercise, I chose a mother at my son's school. I picked the words "judgmental," "critical," and "jealous." The person with characteristics

I admired was Oprah Winfrey. My words for her were "confidence," "bravery," and "empowered." I promise you that I never thought of myself as judgmental or critical or jealous. In fact, those were the very things that I was determined *never* to be. So how could this be in me? I hate to admit it, but I had an internal judge, critic, and insecure wreck living inside who pointed her finger right back at me. My self-judgment and self-criticism was the meanest mean girl on the planet. She would prevent each of my open wounds from healing. My insecurities were great, which made me secretly jealous of others. I would judge the judgers.

Gah! I hated when I learned that. I had to walk toward and face judgment. I had to become judgment, meaning that I had to find it within me. Then I had to love that part of me before I could turn my judgment into discernment.

All negative characteristics have a higher vibration; criticism can turn to praise, and jealousy can turn into admiration. I still admire Oprah and all her valuable gifts, so that means I am slowly, but surely, integrating them into my own body.

If you still need help refining your unique gifts that are powered by your rooted center to become your most authentic primal self, free of fear, loneliness, and doubt, we can call on the goddesses that have sovereignty in this energetic region.

I would like to introduce you to Durga, the Hindu warrioress and protectress goddess, who battles the evils and demonic forces that threaten peace and prosperity. Her name translates into "the invincible one." She looks after cosmic law and order, making sure we choose good over evil. She offers us security as we walk down that corridor of shadows. Durga was born from the male divinities fully grown, and she is the true source of their inner strength. She had primordial powers much greater than the male deities she was birthed from. Durga is usually depicted riding a lion. She has eight arms, each of which holds a special weapon from one of the gods. She is the slayer of shadows and victimization. Durga is an energy that lives within each of us. The mantra *"Om Dum Durgayei Namaha"* honors the powers of protection from Durga, so you can chant the mantra whenever you need to face a fear.

Demeter is the Greek goddess who represents the archetypal nurturing mother. She possesses the mystical powers of an abundant provider of grain and fertility on the earth. In a very short version of Homer's myth, Demeter's daughter Persephone was taken by Hades, who ruled the underworld. Hades cunningly trapped Persephone in the underworld by forcing her to eat pomegranate seeds, which were considered an underworld delight. Seized with grief and rage, Demeter stopped all harvest, growth, and the seasons. Mortals began suffering. When Persephone was eventually allowed to experience the upper world, Demeter rejoiced with sunshine and abundance, thus bringing back spring. Demeter's unconditional and fierce love for her daughter is her love for all daughters. This love provides us with the original source of connection and safety and tribe. Ancient Eleusinian mystery rites honored Demeter and Persephone as initiates to free themselves of the fear of death. Although the rituals are still a mystery, you can eat pomegranates or wear a deep red color to evoke the energies of Demeter and simply call on her nurturing and loving guidance.

Now that you have access to your magical mind and can explore your emotions, your psyche, and your wildest dreams, envision adopting the gifts that the Earth Empress has for you to begin the process of awakening the powers that lie dormant in your root chakra. It shows us our primal magic of worthiness and trust. We must *trust* that we are safe and that the earth is abundant, and we must *know* that we are worthy enough to receive her gifts. That way we feel safe and secure in this world. You have an understanding of your guide animal traits, and you know that you have access to the powerful archetypes of Durga and Demeter to help you face your fears with courage, fierce power, and devoted nurturing. By staying fiercely rooted to Mother Earth's core to access her great wisdom, you can make the choice to awaken the higher-frequency serpent that lay at the foot of the Tree of Life.

As we become more and more rooted to the earth, we experience the Law of Least Effort. This is a cosmic mandate that offers us the ability to *be* and do as your soul intended. Nature does not try to be or act like what it is not. It acts according to its organic state. The caterpillar knows it is a butterfly and takes the steps to become what she truly is. A rose does not compete with the other roses, she is just beauty among beauty.

When we integrate the merged energies of the domesticated woman represented by Eve with the independent woman archetype represented by Lilith, we become unapologetically grounded and expressive, nurturing and fierce, and rooted and wild in love.

{*Lesson: What we judge in others is what we judge in ourselves.*}

CHAPTER 5
Shadow Slayer

The Power of Woman
Seduction of the Senses
Sacred Sexual High Priestess
Shadow Slayer
The Womb of Creation

The Power of Woman

"When sleeping women awake,
mountains will move."
—Chinese Proverb

Whenever I speak in front of a co-ed group, I start out by asking the question, "Who here was born from a woman's body?" Of course, all hands go straight up in the air. And then I will say, "This is just a reminder of the incredible power of women." You already know why I do this, and this is a reminder about the power of *you*.

A patriarchal culture and worldview has vilified and diminished women for *millennia*. Post ancient civilizations when goddess ideology was revered and worshiped, women's circles were dismantled; women became property, women were burnt at the stake, stoned, hanged, raped, labeled the second sex, slut-shamed, and so on. Today, women have to work harder, run faster, pursue more strategically, censor themselves more, and monitor their behavior just to accommodate the patriarchal perspective that women are weaker and less important than men. This long lineage of female bashing makes it hard to shake its negative impact.

We have examples of extraordinary women, like the mother of feminism Gloria Steinem, lawyer and Associate of the U.S. Supreme Court Justice Ruth Bader Ginsburg, Abolitionist Sojourner Truth, poet and activist Audre Lorde, the young Nobel Peace Prize holder Malala Yousafzai, singer/songwriter Taylor Swift, and women represented in movies like *Bombshell*. Each is doing their part to bring awareness to a very sexist culture where the patriarchy still fights for the ideals of separatism, competition, power over, and a zero-sum game of winners and losers – the losers being women. Again and again, I would like to take this opportunity to remind you of a simple fact about the power of woman.

Women, and only women, can create, gestate, and birth life into existence. That is power. The second an egg is fertilized by the male sperm (and yes, we must honor the masculine for seeding this potential), a woman's body becomes an incubator to life. A woman sacredly sacrifices her body in service to life itself. A woman's miraculous body surrenders to this new being growing inside her womb, and her body knows exactly what to do to nourish its growth. A woman's mind, body, and spirit adapt and respond to every single precious evolutionary moment. There are pangs of discomfort and emotional rollercoaster rides as her hips widen, her belly stretches, and her organs get pushed out of the way. All of the food she consumes goes straight to this growing organism first.

Once this new life is completely cooked and ready to be birthed, a woman prepares herself for the ripping apart of her own body. She yields to life's process and collaborates with the human being born through her, thus encouraging their progress together. When the agony and ecstasy of birth itself occurs, she experiences an excruciating pain that she has no choice but to endure.

During her labor, a woman's instincts are heightened and every single part of her body comes alive with extraterrestrial knowledge. The pain at this point is felt in every cell of her muscles, joints, and bones. Her back becomes weakened by the weight of excess fluid and a newly developed separate set of muscles, bones, and flesh inside her. The skin on her belly is so thin now that one can see movement inside, and there is an additional magnitude of pressure on her pelvic floor. Breathing is difficult because her diaphragm is in a different place to make room for this magical being inside her. And when it is time for this miracle to pass through the birth canal, every single emotion, all eighty-eight keys on the piano, is accessed. Every single bit of willpower and love power is used to birth this soul into being. This woman is indifferent to the sweat, tears, and other bodily fluids released from the excretion centers of her body. The pain now is localized, and the burn of being ripped apart is at its most intense. Birth mothers surrender to this heroic process for this incredible new angel, and understand this new soul will soon be on their own separate and sacred path of becoming. The entire time, this woman knows that this new soul will someday leave her.

It does not end there. Once the baby is born, a woman's breasts fill with nourishing milk that sustains the baby and keeps it alive and growing. It happens naturally and on demand. This new mother can instinctually care for the child as they grow into their toddler years and through adolescence. Mothers willingly take the daggers of teenage rebellion, feeling the sorrow of their children's sorrows, and the joys of their joy. The woman, from the beginning, understands that her influence is important for this being to thrive in the world and knows they will separate from her (sometimes unkindly) to create their own magic, in their own way.

No man will ever understand the competence, the sacrifice, the intensity, the weight, the virtue, the devotion, or the unconditional love that is required to birth, nourish, and sustain life. Unless, of course, they begin to honor and respect the very sex that has birthed them into being, and that might not even be enough.

These feminine powers are gifted to all those who honor this feminine divinity within, whether or not you can birth a child, or have yet to birth a child. When you tap into this eternal truth and power within you, the gift of sacred wisdom and divine will is granted.

It is still hard for me to understand the toxic version of masculine energy in some men (and some women), that allows them to discount the dynamic potential and strength of a woman, her magical womb, and the superpowers that are required when she chooses to go through the process of birth in the first place. My beloved feminine divine creatures, this is why the cosmos is asking us to go deeper still, into the cosmic womb of creation, back into the Ocean of Knowing to know the unknowable, to become who we were meant to be, and love beyond how we think we are capable of loving, in order to balance the scales once more. It is time that we all live in harmony, peace, dignity, bliss, rapture, and unconditional love, so we can do our part to resurrect the human race in consciousness. You possess the most divine magic of all... the power of Creation.

{*Lesson: You. Are. Powerful.*}

Seduction of the Senses

"The one who travels like a lover searching
a new passion is suddenly blessed with
new eyes, new ears, new senses"
—Anais Nin

Let's take a dip back into the ocean metaphor. The ocean symbolizes the cleansing of the soul, where pain and loss are washed away, just like our tears are releasing the toxins in our body. The depths of the seas remain a huge mystery, as the depths of our emotions are often a mystery to us. Like the ocean, there are deep crevices that hold an incredible amount of secret wisdom.

The ocean plays a great role in myth and legend. Venus, the goddess of love, was born from the sea. Yemanja is goddess of the ocean and fertility, and also considered the mother of us all, as the source of all the rivers, lakes, and waterways. Water is the symbol of flow and fertility and sensuality. The ocean is the amniotic fluid of the earth, and like the cosmos it is the incubator for all creation. We are made up of mostly water, and all living things need water to survive and thrive. Water is essential, emotional, and sensual. Our sensuality is our senses and sensitivity. We are unconscious without it. When we allow for the seduction of the senses, we open our bodies to subtle senses beyond our recognition, to that magical unknown.

Carl Jung believed the ocean was a mirror to our emotions and the unconscious. The nature of the ocean reflects the depths of our most inner being. The ocean can be both raging with life-threatening tsunamis that consume us, and as peaceful and calming as our first remembrance of safety in the amniotic sac of our mothers. The ocean animal that came to you in the previous transmission is part of your true emotional landscape. Reflect on your sea creature guide again. Can you find commonalities?

Having access to all of your emotions, and learning to identify them so you are not ruled by them but flow with them, is key to understanding the depth and breadth of your soul's desires. It is crucial to exchanging love emotions, sharing vulnerabilities, and experiencing deep intimacy with our partners. We don't often know when an overwhelm of feelings will occur, like anger or sadness or intense love; they simply happen spontaneously depending on the circumstances around us. Emotionality is innate and natural, especially in women. Unfortunately, we live in a culture that fears the truth and fullness of women, so "emotional" is defined in a negative way.

Psychologist Paul Ekman was the first to label six universal emotions found in all humans, in every cultural experience. These emotions were happiness, sadness, disgust, fear, surprise, and anger.

Happiness, or the feelings of joy and contentment, is an emotional experience that is socially accepted. It is the feeling that many of us strive for. Unfortunately, most of the world thinks happiness comes from consumption, but true happiness comes from being fulfilled. And we can't be truly fulfilled unless we know all of the facets of our being. A woman who has access to her joy is positively infectious, she is admired, she is playful, she is radiant. She is constantly inspired by the adventures of life, and teaches her partner how to be romantic.

Sadness, or the feelings of grief and hopelessness, is an emotion that many would rather avoid. But it's from the depth of our sadness that we understand how much we can love and be loved. The author Martín Prechtel writes in his book, *The Smell of Rain on Dust*, that grief is a form of praise. He believes western cultures have difficulty experiencing grief. We've learned to ignore our pain and suffering. We've been asked to tuck our grief neatly away into our emotional hiding places, only to be resolved by our grief haunting us again later. In his book, Prechtel shares tribal rituals of earth cultures that transform grief into life-affirming grace. We must remember how to grieve with reverence. A woman who has access to her sadness is soulful, compassionate, empathetic, and deep. She offers intimacy in relationships, and can awaken a man's heart to love.

Disgust, or the feeling of revulsion, is a reactionary emotion to things that are unpleasant to us. This emotion was originally thought to be an evolutionary response to help humans avoid poisonous foods. A woman who has access to her disgust is brilliant at discernment, has good taste, and has a healthy "no" muscle. In partnerships, she can create necessary boundaries so that both people are individual and free. The couple is defined as two complete individuals who co-create their relationship, and choose to love the common chord of their intersection. They are like two separate circles that come together to create an elliptical center of love. This woman brings the perfect amount of balance and practicality to her relationships.

Fear, as I've already mentioned, is a powerful emotion that causes us to fight, flee, or freeze, and was important to our survival during times of immediate threat. It is fine to have a healthy dose of fear, but we cannot let fear have us. A woman who can access her fear in a productive way can be mysterious, bashful, humble, and quite frankly smart enough to get out of harm's way. As a lover, she can be tantalizing, seductive, and creative.

Surprise is an emotional startle response following something unexpected, good, bad, or neutral. It is adorable to watch a baby in surprise. The surprise may result in rapturous laughter or a cry, but that moment of surprise is precious. A woman with access to the emotion of surprise is full of wonder and curiosity, she is youthful, innocent, flirtatious, and in flow. She disarms even the harshest of critics, and her relationships are always fresh and explorative. There is no boredom with a woman who is full of awe.

Anger is another powerful emotion that feels like hostility, frustration, and aggression toward others. It is also part of the fight-or-flight response. This is seen as a negative emotion in our culture as well, but we do need to release our anger so that it does not stay in our bodies and erupt outwards toward another. Many therapeutic modalities teach the proper expression of anger, like beating on pillows or screaming in the woods. With too many injustices in the world, it would be unhealthy to lock up our anger. It is the unleashing of our sacred rage that releases the energy of transformation. A woman who has access to her rage is fierce, energetic, magnetic, influential, confident, and the first to champion the underdog. She loves her partner fiercely, stands for their relationship, and is a passionate lover.

Ekman's theory first suggested the six basic emotions and identified them by facial expressions. But they are just pieces of the puzzle to our emotional depths. Many other theories continue to research the various types of emotions we experience, like my favorite feeling, love, which we will get to in depth later. Ekman later added other emotions to his list, not all classified with facial expressions. They include amusement, contentment, excitement, contempt, embarrassment, relief, pride, guilt, satisfaction, and, of course, shame.

Shame. Let's talk about shame. More specifically, let's talk about the feminine shame that is held in our emotional power center. Feminine shame is the shame or shaming of sensuality and sexuality. It is the shaming of our power as women. Lilith, banished for being independent, was turned into the cause of all sexual harlotry. Eve, who is portrayed as the first sinner, offers us sexual shame by being the good girl gone bad for not listening to the rules. In every single society today, we as sexual women are crucified by the very act and energy that creates, gestates, births, and sustains life.

Therefore, our emotional power center is the most important area for women to activate. It holds the fuel of transformation, it awakens the serpent life-force energy that activates all other power centers in our body, and it holds our symbolic ocean of knowing. It is the place where we feel emotions for ourselves, and connects us to the emotions of others. When this area is blocked, we are blocked from the felt sense of our beauty, our power, our sacred rage, our joy, our grief, and everything in between. If we do not have access to our emotions, we do not have access to embodied wisdom, because embodied wisdom *requires* feeling.

{*Lesson: You have permission to feel...everything.*}

Sacred Sexual High Priestess

> "The erotic is a measure between
> the beginnings of our sense of self
> and the chaos of our strongest
> feelings. It is an internal sense of
> satisfaction to which, once we have
> experienced it, we know we can aspire"
> —Audre Lorde

Welcome to the sacral chakra, the home of the Cosmic Law of Intention and Desire, where the Holy Grail has been hiding right under our noses. I'm sure you guessed that our elemental guide is water. Her sensual current guides us to your hidden magic. The divine beings of Isis, Mary Magdalene, Venus, and Kali come to us in this womb space of creation, where eroticism, desires, and the power of manifestation exist. These divine feminine love archetypes know the process of alchemy and the transforming of shadow into light.

The Holy Grail is our Feminine Power, our sexual power. It is a spiritual force used for awakening us to higher dimensions. When we awaken this energy fully, we can manifest anything. This is the foundation of what Isis, Magdalene, and Kundalini teach – to free our sexual energy from being held in the lower chakras and bring it up through the higher chakras for an elevated expression of co-creation.

In this sacred space, we will also honor our inner prostitute before elevating her to Divine Lover. Ancient mystery schools believed Magdalene was a student of Isis. Both archetypes have come back into the modern collective psyche to help us reach the heights of our feminine spirituality – in this lifetime. Today, many more seers, oracles, and spiritual guides are tapping into this wisdom. As I mentioned, Magdalene has come to me before, and I look forward to her visits again. Her message to me was simple: our divinity lives in the temple of our bodies, our sexual bodies. Eroticism is simply a spiritually and sensually awakened essence, unashamed of the magnitude of life-force energy it exudes. Giving yourself permission to experience your sacred sexuality allows you to be fully embodied with the creative force of divinity. Desire, passion, polarity, intention, and surrender are the erotic qualities of creation. If you recall from the beginning of time, Consciousness had the desire and intention to express itself, and so the polarity and friction within the space of no-thing that passionately exploded into the everything, has this same erotic energy beneath it. When we know that everything around us is a reflection of ourselves on a macro-level as the divine spirit, and on a micro-level as soul, human, mother, and woman, we walk the path of Heaven on Earth without a drop of shame.

Sadly, the low-vibrational man is so afraid of his potential impotence, this very power in women is abused, raped, criticized, shamed, and labeled as a prostitute. Again, this has been going on for too long. Magdalene's embodiment of the sacred feminine and her wisdom of Kundalini energy was later translated into something very different. Those that edited out key sacred texts from the Bible could not imagine that Jesus would view a woman as his equal, so they demoted Magdalene to be a lowly prostitute – the vilification of women repeating itself once again. Missing from the Bible is the Gospel of Mary, which was found in 1896 in Egypt and is the only written text attributed to a woman prophet. In it, Mary Magdalene is portrayed as a prominent disciple of Jesus and the only witness to his resurrection, making Magdalene a very important part of religious history as a spiritual equal.

During my meditations when both Mother Mary and Magdalene come to me at the same time, I see their archetypal message as a reminder of the deliberate splitting apart of womanhood by the patriarchy, and the need to reclaim both energies within each of us. I am sure you have heard of the "Madonna-Whore" complex? Sigmund Freud suggests that men with this complex have a hard time maintaining their sexual arousal in their monogamous, intimate partnerships because their wives are the women they see as the pure and nurturing Mother Mary (Madonna) type. They replace their sexual desire for women who have been disgraced in some way (Whore), to feel hero-like, which satisfies an unseen primal part of their own sexuality, and to validate a sexual hierarchy. "Where such men love they have no desire, and where they desire they cannot love," Sigmund Freud wrote.

In the book *When God Was a Woman*, art historian and sculptor Merlin Stone suggests that patriarchal rule tried to edit out the validity of a goddess-based culture during Sumerian times where men, through the rituals of Sacred Marriage, attained the privilege of becoming custodians to the peoples of the goddess Inanna. This is another example where the High Priestesses were demoted to prostitutes farther back in history to diminish the power of women. The many years of a woman's sexuality being labeled as negative has implications to our psyche. It makes us feel like we have to give ourselves away just to placate the unconscious masculine.

According to Carl Jung, we all have the prostitute archetype in us, a shadow aspect that developed from this historic diminishment of a woman's power. It shows up whenever we "sell our souls" for something, or "sell ourselves short." It does not mean that you have a habit of walking the streets after dark and selling your body for money. But we've all chosen to put our own truths aside for a job, or a partner, or an experience. Have you ever done this?

I have had to endure the backlash of awakening to my truest essence as a woman. The people in my life who had the remnants of a dominating, patriarchal worldview battled to keep control over what is innately wild and free in me: my emotionality, my sensuality, my sexuality, my intuition, my feminine divinity, and the desire to create (in my way) a platform to spread love wisdom. It was like they were trying to tame the ocean and put it in a box. It is impossible to tame the ocean. The key for me (and for those on the path of awakening) was to own every single bit of this goddess nectar that is generated from within the sacral chakra, shapeshift with energies of the feminine deity archetypes, own my shadows so I could recognize their shadows with radical acceptance, and love them through the process of dismantling the systems that tried to keep me small and invisible. I will admit, to be punished for being a woman who lives her truth is not easy.

The many occult ideologies that believe both Mother Mary and Mary Magdalene were students in the Isis mystery schools, gives us a fuller picture of these two powerful women. Isis is known to be the most dynamic goddess of sexual magic and power, who resurrected her husband Osiris from the dead. She is another goddess of a thousand names from which all other Egyptian goddesses emerged. Isis is said to be the one who gave birth to Heaven and

Earth. Many representations of snakes in conjunction with Isis are symbols of this serpent energy that awakens from its coiled up slumber in the root chakra, and rises to stimulate the magnetic force in the sacral chakra and each of the other power centers thereafter. In ancient Egypt, Greek, and other esoteric philosophies, this energy is known to be the divine sacred essence of Creation herself.

If you are currently going through some challenges, or have had your share of challenges throughout your life and feel like you need a resurrection, this is a sign that you are in the crucible of initiation with Isis. She wants you to wake up. Her gifts to you are these life tests for advanced spiritual growth and the capacity to love wildly and courageously. She is asking you to look for the light in the deepest crevices of your emotional caves to stir your inner serpent.

Magdalene who was witness to Jesus' resurrection and Isis who resurrected Osiris from the dead, are sacred sexual high priestesses who have initiated me (and now you) in the understanding that our bodies and our sexuality are to be revered. A woman, once awakened, can give this feminine wisdom to men by resurrecting the divine masculine within herself first. It cannot happen the other way around. Men cannot teach a woman about her feminine genius, and it is the awakened energy of the divine feminine that will bring spiritual balance to the divine masculine.

This kind of power is why we have been demoted in the Garden of Eden to the level of sin. Re-activating our serpent power and alchemizing all of our wounds back into their higher-octave potential, transports us into the divine feminine sanctuary of embodied wisdom. We do this through the integration of our subtle body emotions and our full-body sensations.

Setting free our lower-octave feelings of guilt, jealousy, shame, and even low-vibrational desires, and transforming our sacred wounds and the seven deadly sins will free us to feel the higher vibrations of grace, bliss, gratitude, ecstasy, and romantic love.

{Lesson: The Holy Grail is hidden within you.}

Shadow Slayer

"The path to paradise begins in hell."
—Dante Alighieri

The first step to opening up to your sensuality is to get rid of any sensual blocks that may inhibit you from completely *feeling* alive. This could be anything from being confused by society's messages to deeper childhood wounds. As mentioned before, the "Madonna-Whore" paradox is deeply ingrained in our society. We are either whores or mothers. We can't be both.

When we are single, we try a little harder to be attractive so that we may find a partner. This is a natural custom that many cultures practice. We also see it in nature and the animal kingdom. Birds are drawn to beautiful flowers and animals (mostly males, like peacocks) are adorned with bright-colored feathers to attract a mate. But after we commit to monogamy, get married, and have children, some of us get a little lazy about our "attractiveness." We also get pigeonholed into the mother archetype, which is about nurturing and pleasing. We choose to give up on our sensuality, or are too exhausted to feel it, especially if our lovers can't accept both energies in us. When you make sensuality a daily practice, you get to a point where you can flow with the perfect amount of sensuality needed at any moment. Sensuality, or our sensitivity, is necessary for the body to feel her desires.

If knowing what you desire is still hard, then it is time to dissolve the blocks from the painful experiences you might still be holding on to, be it a bad breakup, affair, divorce, abuse, shaming or guilt for being who you are. To help us find these blocks, let's descend together again into the shadows of the seven deadly sins.

I would like to invite the goddess Kali to join us as our guide this time. Kali is the fierce Hindu goddess representing the continuous feminine rhythm of death and destruction, life and rebirth, chaos and creativity. Understanding her gifts before we react to situations can help us understand the unpredictability and spontaneity of our own behavior. She helps us turn the rage in ourselves (and in others) into fierce love.

The legendary Hindu tale of Kali begins with the war between the demon Raktabija and the goddess Durga. Any time a drop of Raktabija's blood hit the earth, it turned into another demon. The battle was so intense that Durga in her rage burst forth the form of Kali from the center of her forehead. Once born, Kali, the black goddess, went ravenous and devoured all the demons she came across, stringing their heads on a chain that she wore around her neck. Every drop of blood spilled by the wounded Raktabija that became a deadly fighting clone, Kali would victoriously slay. As the numbers increased and the battle intensified, she turned it around and defeated Raktabija by swallowing all of his blood before it touched the ground, then devoured the remaining replicate demons.

This ability to slay demons and drink their blood is the power of destroying the demons in our psyche. The power of Kali is the key to inner psychic freedom and letting go into chaos. She is not just the slayer of demons, but also our ego. Kali represents absolute Reality. She is the one who helps us destroy the constructs that hide our true identity.

I introduce Kali here because she often comes to us in the form of our hidden and mostly terrifying chaotic situations that have to do with shame and fear and guilt as women. When we tap into her creative and cathartic force, we can use her fearless energy to become aware of how we have given away our own powers, and gain the courage to uplift our repressed and oppressed shadows into a higher vibration. We enter the dance of our own dark reality and begin the true transformation toward the light. When we are unconscious of our path through life, Kali is the one who will throw the bricks at our faces, asking us to pay attention and wake up. Fortunately, or unfortunately, I have a very close relationship to Kali energy.

To invoke Kali, you must be willing to surrender to her will. Like a fierce mother, she will guide you straight into the furnace of middle earth and show you how to transform the seven deadly sins that hold you back from loving and living at your highest potential. It was she who first came to you in your time of suffering, provoking and taunting you with what you feared most. She does not do this out of hatred, but from Unconditional Love. She offers us wisdom on transformation, and she shares with us how to transcend the ego. If we choose to ignore her, she will come to us with greater force. I know this from experience. You might too.

Kali brings together the alchemical fire from our solar plexus and the erotic essence from our sacral chakra to transform our guilt, greed, shame, envy, and the other deadly sins into their higher frequencies of right action, generosity, self-love, confidence, and so on. As you recall, the steps to transforming our fears are to face your fears, look at them with curiosity up close and personal, then become your fears and know that they are part of you, just hidden in the shadows. From there you can transform them through the kiss of love.

"*Om Krim Kali*" is the mantra that helps protect us from all evils. Say it out loud a few times to try it on. The vibrational sounds invoke Kali. Now imagine the dark goddess, often depicted with blue skin, and long black, disheveled hair. Her wide-open fiery eyes can see through eternity. See her tongue hanging from her mouth, dripping with blood. Close your eyes and see this image.

Allow your mind to be free of thought as you read the following words. Scan your body from head to toe, sensing the wholeness of your physicality. Is there a part of your body that feels tight, or hollow, or throbbing? Put your hand on that place. If you feel like there is something blocking that space, imagine what that blockage looks like. Is it a cork, a string, a stone, maybe a hole covered with a thin layer of papyrus? Feel free to close your eyes any time to imagine and tap into the felt sense of this invocation. With your mind's eye, remove the covering or blockage in your body, and enter through it. Make your way down to the sacral chakra, the space between your pubic bone and your belly button. This is the magical and mysterious womb space. Kali awaits you with her swords and the skulls of the many demon heads hung around her neck. She whispers in your ears a secret to navigating the darkness. Close your eyes again and imagine what she says to you, specifically you.

If nothing comes to you, do not worry. Your subconscious has been activated to uncover the secret tools you need; simply trust that it will come to you at the perfect moment, maybe in your dreams tonight. Imagine this space you've entered to be dark and cavernous with many different secret entryways. You pick the one closest to you, go toward the opening and step deeper inside. Your eyes slowly adjust to the darkness of this hallow den to find the silhouette of someone near the back wall, reclining on the cold floor with tragic laziness. Sloth is her name. Her hair is unkempt, her fingers dirty, her clothes wrinkled. She might even smell a little. Kali is about to slay her with her sword, but you recognize that it is you in the corner. This is disturbing. You watch in amazement as Kali walks over to Sloth and slices off her head. You immediately feel a tightness around your neck as you watch Sloth's ego fall to the floor. Kali turns to you and tells you that the mycelium of the earth is already doing their job to transform Sloth's inert qualities into diligence, purpose, liveliness, and the fruit of knowledge. Sloth will now take right action toward love and fulfillment. Take in a breath now and observe the scene with open curiosity, then ask yourself what part of you is failing to act on your most innate gifts. Are you, in any way, apathetic to your spiritual growth and personal empowerment?

Kali then guides you deeper into a crack in the cave wall that has less light. It feels wet and sticky there. As the space opens up, you see Lust standing in the middle of the room, half-naked with her breasts exposed. She is shameless and seductive as she pleasures herself into orgasmic rapture, her ravenous desires never fulfilled. She begs to know your most erotic desires. She wants and wants and wants. You again recognize the resemblance to you. Do you feel any embarrassment now? Do you feel any shame now? Ask yourself if you still have dreams and desires yet unmet. Are you yearning for soul love, or is your intent for divine purpose still unclear?

Kali takes her sword and puts it through the belly of Lust, and you watch the transformation of yearning into the truth that we have everything that we need inside us; the power of creation, purity, a sacredness for this life-force energy, and the sensual powers of water. Lust becomes Love, and she is now able to give the qualities of love and sensuality to her partner in an equal rhythm that is fulfilling, not depleting.

Kali then guides you to a fiery light. It is uncomfortably hot and you begin to sweat. Kali begins a rageful dance to summon Wrath, who seems to be hiding in the corner. This being has been waiting and waiting to unleash her rage at the untruths and injustices that keep punching her in the face, a face that resembles yours. She cannot stop the feeling of the betrayals, the estrangement, the alienation, the abuse done to you or to others or to the planet. She recognizes that she too has done damage to others through her wild temperament. Wrath is unleashed through Kali and she wants to burn the earth down. Are there people or circumstances in your life that still need your forgiveness? Are there resentments you have not let go of yet? You watch this battle of Wrath and Rage, unable to detect who will win. And then you watch as Kali consumes the whole of Wrath, and Wrath is gone. The blood dripping from Kali's lips touches the ground to become Equanimity who embodies patience, protection, compassion, grace, and the gifts of fire power.

Kali's palate wet, she is restless with anticipation to meet yet another worthy opponent, Pride. Kali loves to slay the ego of Pride. You watch the arrogant Pride standing tall and boastfully on a foundation of insecurity, uncertainty, and self-doubt. She holds a mirror to make sure she is in perfect presentation for others. She brags loudly in the mirror about how much better she is than others. Where in your life do you need to practice humility and tenderness? Are there areas in your life where you still feel insecure? Kali splits Pride in half with her sword, and she immediately turns into Empowerment. She now can practice the magic of sovereignty, humility, service, support, and charm.

You then follow Kali deeper still to the place where Greed is sitting on a pile of coins and jewels, like a dragon sits on its stolen treasures. She counts her money over and over again, while attending to her material goods. It is not enough. It is never enough. She takes and takes and takes and takes. She has no regard for the earth or the cosmos or her spiritual growth. She continually references outward, always wanting what she does not have, simply because she does not have it. She is the betrayer of women, the "other woman" of infidelity. Where and when do you hold back your love or from love? Are you being guided by lack or abundance? Do you fear that you do not have enough, or that you are not enough? Kali does not harm Greed. Instead she burns all of her belongings and her wealth into ashes, until Greed has nothing left but herself. Through Greed's torment blossoms generosity, charity, kindness, and earth's magic. She becomes Abundance.

Finally, Kali guides you to the last of the seven deadly sinners, Envy. Envy is beautiful yet very cruel. Beneath her allure, she judges, criticizes, and blames others for everything that she is denied. Envy talks behind peoples' backs, and puts them down with lies or half-truths. Her jealousy is masked with a saccharine smile and passive-aggressive style of communicating. Are there people in your life who are competitive with you, or you with them? Do you judge or criticize others, or do you judge yourself? Kali uses her sword to slowly and methodically slice the skin off of Envy's entire body so she is left with fascia, muscle, and bone, leaving her with no outward identity. Envy is at her most vulnerable before she transforms into Generosity. She now exemplifies self-confidence, gratitude, good-will, admiration, blessings, and the magical quality of seeing beyond the veil of perception.

You and Kali finally take refuge in the purified womb space of creation, where she tells you the truth about sins and sinners. Because the Universe does not see anything as good or bad, she tells you, a sin is simply the shadow side of a virtue that is meant to challenge us into making choices that elevate our souls to a higher realm, or bring it down to a lower level. No choice is good or bad, it is simply an experience in one way or another that has consequences, or karma. They are an opportunity for us to feel contrast so that we can learn more. If we can admit to the shadow qualities in us, we diminish their power over us. We would not be interested in the tales of good and evil if we did not have the potential for both inside us. Your choice is to transform what you feel inhibits you, and awaken yourself to what brings you pleasure. The feeling of pleasure, and all our felt senses for that matter, comes from the sacral chakra. Kali kisses you on the forehead, and whispers in your ear that she is you, the power of fierce love and transformation within, and then melts into your skin.

As you begin to let go and release all the shame, guilt, and fears that are no longer in service to your highest potential to love and be loved, to serve, to create, and to simply *be*, you will start the process toward emptiness. This emptiness will create a magnetic pull to all things that are sacredly abundant, beautiful, sensual, creative, life-affirming, and peaceful. So forgive yourself, gorgeous and divine troublemaker. Your soul simply had a plan to exercise her wings and give herself a good challenge worthy of ascension.

{*Lesson: You have badass in you.*}

Womb of Creation

The womb of creation is where we rebirth you as Goddess. A little secret revealed now is that you have *all* the energies of *all* the goddesses within you, including the goddess resurrected from the foamy seas, Venus. Perhaps this is the first time you have considered yourself an alluring, dazzling, and mesmerizing Goddess of Love. Or maybe it's the perfect time to elevate and refine your description to include abundance, self-worth, and exquisite beauty to your definition of yourself, and all women.

Venus is embedded in our psyche through art, music, poetry, and the mythological stories about her. She is the Roman goddess who defines Love, Beauty, Desire, Sex, Fertility, Prosperity, and Victory at the highest level of vibration. Her mythology was so important that the Roman Emperor Julius Caesar claimed Venus as an ancestress, and so became the Mother of Rome. The Romans believed that she was the same as Aphrodite in Greek mythology and adopted some of her symbols, such as roses, myrtle, pearls, and mirrors, to worship her. Both were born from seafoam. Even the planet Venus was named after the goddess, for it is so radiant and beautiful in the night sky that the astronomers of antiquity felt this bright star worthy of the beautiful and radiant goddess. Venus in your astrological charts will tell you what kind of romantic lover you are and where your innate gifts to create and experience beauty lie.

As we continue on our journey from understanding our primal nature and powers, the ideal of Venus can emerge from the depths of the emotional and sensual realm. Reclamation of your inner love-beauty goddess through your intimate connection with the world, and the witnessing of yourself in a more exalted light is in order. We have tapped into the depths of your emotional well-being, and now it is time to rise from those waters with naked truth and dazzling radiance.

Rising into the Venus archetype is an opportunity to find clarity on how much self-love, abundance, and inner beauty we feel and see for ourselves. The self-love we have is a reflection of the kind of loving relationships that are magnetized to us; the more abundant we feel, the more abundance is offered to us; and the more beauty we see inside us will radiate through us as a reflection of the beauty that surrounds us.

Self-love is something to be cultivated and we will cultivate it as Venus would. Your emotions should never be judged; instead, they should be felt and expressed fully, then let go. Self-care is understanding that you are the most important person to care for *first*. If you lack self-love, nourishment, feeling pampered and filled up, you cannot love, nourish, pamper, or fill up those who are important to you. We can only share what we have, so your goal is to be overflowing with self-love so that you can share it with others. See your self-care as a sacred act.

During my Ayurvedic educator training, we were expected to go through the Chopra Center's *Perfect Health* program as part of the certification process. It was the ultimate in self-care, mind, body, soul, and spirit. We did yoga, meditated, attuned to nature, ate nourishing meals, experienced various types of daily massages, and learned the ancient wisdom of life. Yes, *every day* we experienced a heavenly and nourishing massage. If you don't have the time to make self-care vacations a habit, simply list all the things you can do for yourself to feel more self-love now. Make it a habit to do at least one act of self-care, like looking in the mirror and giving yourself a kind compliment every day, and one "luxurious" act once a week (this could mean relaxing and reading a good book for an hour in your robe and slippers). Self-care is self-awareness. Fine-tuning and attending to your instrument of life, the body, becomes a sensual experience of the world around you. As Oscar Wilde says, "To love oneself is the beginning of a life-long romance."

I have a practical and easy exercise to offer you, and that is to give yourself a love bubble bath, or rather a lovely Venus bath. Venus was born from seafoam, and we are born from the waters of our mother's wombs. Creating a rebirthing experience with ceremony and ritual provides a sanctuary from which your psyche and emotions can safely honor the forward momentum you are creating for yourself. A little celebration every time you've transcended a critical mind block, gives juice to your growth and will help keep you dancing toward your higher goals. The Venus bath is a luxurious experience and celebration worthy of a goddess.

Draw yourself a bath that includes rose petals, candles, music, and bubbles. Honey and milk can be added to the water when the water is filling up to make your bath frothy like seafoam. The milk and honey are nourishing for your skin. If you wish, you can add a scent of patchouli oil (uplifting), lavender oil (relaxation), or jasmine (sensual). Text two or more really good friends just before you get into the tub and ask them to share with you five things that are special about you. Copy this phrase if you need to: "I was given this exercise to ask if you would share with me five words that that make me special. Thanks (add appropriate emoji)." Then put the phone away and forget you did that.

Before you step into the bath, make a promise to yourself to stop negative thoughts about your body, your mind, and your soul. Say to yourself, "I no longer diminish myself. I love myself unconditionally, and through unconditional love I will call in the love, the beauty, and the abundance that I deserve. So be it." Then step into the bath. Relax, enjoy, and let the water melt away any residual emotional toxins. Do not expect anyone to send you back a text immediately. Simply enjoy your bath and your time alone with the most magnificent person on the planet – you.

After this magical bath, your body will be open to receiving more information from the cosmos. And because our bodies are receptors of information and communicators of our souls, it is also valuable to add movement and be fluid in our movement. If emotions are energy in motion, then the movement of our bodies unlock the rigid and negative thoughts and emotional patterns that get stuck in the fascia and muscles.

The late Stanley Keleman, therapist and pioneer of formative psychology, says that "the body is a living, creative process. Our bodies are an expression in microcosm of the creative organizing principle of the Universe." He studied the connection of the body with emotional, sexual, psychological, and imaginative states. Because our natural expression is to continually form and reform sexual, emotional, psychological, and imaginative elements of our human experience, this somatic-emotional approach helps us discover our individual patterns, offering us a better reality of Self.

I visited Stanley Keleman a few times in his offices in Berkeley, California before I started my journey of awakening. My intention was to understand why I was so frozen in my body, which kept me from my ability to feel and thus my ability to know what

I wanted from my experience through life. I was the typical good girl pleaser who tried to do everything "right." It was a survival skill I learned at birth. When Stanley asked me to walk across the room a couple of times, I stood tall and composed and walked as straight as I could to the wall and back. He told me that I should walk casually, as if I were walking with friends, and I did it again, just more slowly. I was very impressed with myself. I thought he was going to tell me that I had impeccable posture and walked a perfectly straight line. Instead, he told me that I had an adolescent walk. My arms were stiff, and my hips did not sway in a natural flow with side-to-side motion as a mature woman's body should. He was right, I never felt confident enough to walk boldly and naturally in the world like that. I was afraid of being "too much," or worse, taken advantage of.

Another time that I saw him, we sat across from each other conversing casually before he asked me to "be at ease." I told him I was relaxed. I sat as I always sat, with my back straight and sitz bones even against the seat of the chair (again, great posture). I didn't realize that I was holding my breath or that I always held my breath in front of authority figures. He was over six feet tall, a big man in his eighties, and a doctor. That was authority enough for me. He suggested that if I took a deep breath in, exhaled slowly, and relaxed my pelvic floor, it would help me be more at ease. That request so perplexed me. Why would anyone relax their pelvic floor? I told him that if I did let my pelvic floor relax, I might wet my pants. He pointed to a box of Kleenex and said we could wipe it up in the unlikely chance that happened. So I relaxed my pelvic floor. My body, instead of looking like a soldier on call, settled in just a little more, but it made the biggest difference in how I presented myself. I was still in good posture, but not as "uptight."

I looked gracefully composed and at ease. "That looks much better," he said. "How does it feel?"

Oddly, it didn't feel good to me at all. I felt slouchy, messy, slovenly even, though I was still maintaining good posture. I felt like my father during his darkest years after a long night of drinking and gambling, asleep in front of the flickering television with a lit cigarette in his mouth. And then I made an irritated gesture with my hands, holding them over my head with my fingers splayed apart. I told Stanley how much it bothered me to feel slumped like my father in that way (even though my posture was aligned). And that was what he was looking for, the gesture that told him how much energy I was vigilantly holding in my body that kept me armored with rigid protection. When he had me drop my energetic defenses, I cried a torrential rain of tears, because I did not have the barricades up to protect myself from any violent outburst that I thought might happen at any moment. This was my first experience of knowing that our pains hide in our nervous system, fascia, and muscles. We can break the patterns of negative thoughts and actions through somatic practices of moving the body: yoga, running, swimming, biking, walking, and especially dancing with unchoreographed and non-linear motion are great ways to do this.

With the right intention, movement can also help transform the way we feel about ourselves because our emotions are just energy in motion. The release of overpowering feelings through dance or exercise is very beneficial for our self-worth and confidence. Movement can be the perfect cathartic experience that allows our bodies to surrender enough to let go of what we cannot control. The vitality we experience from movement, especially dance, heightens our senses, and enlivens our erotic bodies with the feel-good memories needed for manifestation. With this clarity, we can consider the refinement of our desires to include more intention and attention. Which brings us back to our desires, love, and the Law of Detachment.

Surrender is a principle teaching of detachment. When we have a desire to find a soulmate, create something important in the world, or want to be the most that we can be, the practice of detachment to the outcome is what makes space for the Universe to conspire on our behalf. When we surrender to *what is* and release control over every minute detail of our desires, it anchors in the certainty of our trust in the extraordinary wisdom of divine law. This is essential. When we surrender to uncertainty and simply let go, we are committing to the divine unfolding of miracles within us and for us. We are left with a deep sense of freedom and security. The feeling in the bath and the feeling after you've released tension in the body to its most relaxed state is the feeling of surrender.

Give yourself permission to melt into all of who you are: the wild woman, sensual lover, bold leader, timid ingénue, expressive Creatrix, kind mother, super warrioress. Accept others as they are. Surrender incites spontaneous opportunities and solutions and manifestations.

{Lesson: Radical Self-Care is essential to Radical Self-Love,
which is essential to Soulmating.}

CHAPTER 6

Holy Warrioress

The Pyramid of Light
Animal Magnetism
Predator or Prey?
Holy Warrioress

The Pyramid of Light

Pyramids, temples, and archaic structures like Stonehenge are a great wonder and a deep mystery for those of us who are curious to know the meaning and power behind the creation of such magnificent infrastructures. The study of pyramidology suggests that the ancient astronomers of Egypt built the pyramids to align with the rising and the setting of the stars, specifically Sirius. "*Seirios*," the Greek word meaning "scorcher" or "glowing," became the name "Sirius," the brightest and most resplendent of all the twinkling stars in the sky. Apparently, Sirius has great influence on our weather; astronomers claim that it influences the heat of our sun to give us the "dog days of summer." To many ancient civilizations, the light of Sirius also represents the most exalted light of truth and meaningful service to others, which can be translated into our highest potential.

Sumerian and Babylonian cultures revered Sirius as a display of sacred messages from the heavens, connecting the great light with Source energy itself. The celestial movements of the stars were used to predict events here on Earth by the astronomers-astrologers of that time. As mentioned before, the ancient Egyptians associated the star Sirius with the goddess Isis to signal when the flooding of the Nile river was near. The creation myth of the Nile river tells the story of Isis shedding a river of tears while mourning the death of her husband Osiris. This mythology connects the star's meaning to sacrifice, devotion, powerful magic, feminine energy, perseverance, fertility, and hope. The metaphor of Sirius as a celestial goddess is one who radiates authentic power to all those who are devoted to cultivating this love force within themselves, and empowering love in others.

Since you are still reading these words (thank you, by the way), take this as a sign that your vibration is ready to blast into another dimension of fabulousness with the help of Sirius and the warrioress archetypes who wield the power of light and alchemy.

Welcome, Holy Warrioress, to the Pyramid of Light, where power, grace, animal magnetism, passion, and purpose are activated in this dynamic center. This Pyramid of Light lies in the solar plexus, located in the pit of your stomach. In Sanskrit, it is called the "*Manipura* chakra," meaning "resplendent gem." Biologically, the solar plexus is a bunch of complex connections of nerves and ganglia, which activate the fight-or-flight response in the sympathetic nervous system. You may feel it as a "gut reaction," or your animal instincts. Energetically, this center is your direct connection with the energy of the Sun in our solar system, and the star of Sirius beyond it, to offer you a raw and potent electromagnetic power.

Each of us has a unique ray of light that includes the fuel from our past and past life karma. As more and more of the fears and shames buried in the root chakra are transformed into fuel, they can be integrated into your unique ray of light that includes your personal desires, passions, and the hidden and forbidden selves found in the sacral chakra. When the Buddha talks about inner peace, he does not suggest that you have to go outside yourself to get it. Inner peace is releasing the anger, fear, or resentments that we hold inside to block us from our truest essence of harmony and love. The alchemy in this fiery power center helps transform the guilt and judgment of your shadow self into the prism of your radiant self. In the Pyramid of Light, we connect to our one-of-a-kind power to become extraordinarily empowered. To be empowered is the only way to empower or lead others. It is our gut knowing of what is aligned with your soul essence that gives you your unquestionable "yes" and your "no" for any choices you need to make.

In his book *Power versus Force,* Dr. David Hawkins writes, "Transcendence of the personal self and surrender to the very essence or spirit of life often occurs at a point just beyond the apparent limit of one's ability." In this passage, he is referring to the heroine within, who is required to overcome limiting beliefs and a societal system that keeps her from achieving the highest level of her prowess. Higher states of consciousness can be attained as you transcend the obstacles on your journey through life, access the strength and will within you, *and* connect to the divine wisdom that is there (if you want it) to guide you on your odyssey.

Spontaneous higher states of consciousness, often experienced by athletes or those who acquire the impulsive strength or abilities to save another person from a dangerous situation – like the mother who lifts up a car to save her child, or the athlete who breaks a world record – are zones of effortless bliss and peak performance. The prima ballerina as she twirls and jumps and lifts her legs into the sky and the musician who keeps creating and sharing her music are examples of tapping into this zone to embody the intensity of power...with grace and with calm.

We all have the ability to experience this quality of infinite potential and eternal fierce love, though it does require the activation of the Law of Least Resistance. The Law of Least Resistance includes practice, preparation, intention, and trusting your body memory to act and react with ease and flow. It is like doing a yoga posture where you are asked to stretch your body in all directions, extending the energy beyond your extremities, activating all of your muscles, and then finally having to *relax* in the pose.

The solar plexus chakra is also where you understand your *doing* in the world, and where we consider *doing* only after the art of *Being*. Remember, the Arc of Being that I mentioned earlier in this book is to first *know* who you are at your highest potential. This helps you to awaken the multidimensional and multifaceted soul and integrate these energies in your human body to *be* your highest and whole self in the world. Unfortunately, you cannot create like a Creatrix, or love like a Lover, or lead like a Leader, unless you embody those qualities first. If you don't first believe in the reality of your exalted, magnificent, ever-so-mighty self, no one else will either. The *"fake it 'til you make it"* trick does not work. You must actualize the *whole* sacred, magical, powerful you in order to realize it. Radical acceptance, and therefore radical self-love, is the action and reaction in response to the divine alignment of your highest self with your desires, your soul's purpose, your service, and your love vortex. We alchemize these qualities of the Holy Warrioress in this spectrum of light and vibration. When you step into your authentic power, the Law of Least Resistance can be known.

It is time to summon a few warrior goddesses who hold supremacy in this radiant Pyramid of Light energy. We will be calling on Isis, Bastet, Sekhmet, and Athena. The personification of these archetypes are not as untamed as the protectress Durga or her sacred assassin offspring Kali. The energy here is majestic, unflappable, confident, poised, undisputable, the heroine's journey realized. In "real" life, these are the feminine leaders, boss babes, and women on the front lines of the global health crises, who have no doubt about their purpose and power and passion.

With the intention for ease, efficiency, and co-creation with your divine plan, we are going to enter your Pyramid of Light to find your weapons of empowerment, love, and truth. We will use the ancient symbol of the pyramid as related to the soul and the love trinity. Isis rules the Pyramids of Light to energize them with her magnificent magic. Joining us on our journey is Bastet, an ancient solar and war cat goddess said to embody the soul of Isis. Her feline intuition and sensual dexterity balances the ferocity of her sister Sekhmet, goddess of the sun, war, destruction, and healing. While Bastet is depicted as a cat, Sekhmet is the lioness. Athena, the goddess of wisdom and warcraft, is the energy of feminine courage, ingenuity, and justice. Part of Athena's legend is that she turned the once beautiful Medusa into the snake-headed Gorgon monster. Athena's powers are not to be reckoned with. Sampling this kind of energy within you is to champion yourself and the underdogs who might need your encouragement and inspiration at any given moment. The personification of this energy is activating the Wonder Woman within you.

It is worth reminding you here that this process of Magical Mind Shaping is scientifically-based. Cognitive scientists at Dartmouth College studied how the neural network of our "mental workplace" across many regions of the brain helps us come up with creative thought and imagination. Seeing things from various perspectives to learn and create new concepts has a lot to do with our vibrant and varied "mental playground." In his podcast series *Infinite Potential,* Deepak Chopra says that "the rewiring of your brain is a result of neuroplasticity, which includes two things: Neurogenesis (the growth of new neurons) and synaptogenesis (new connections between neurons). You can enhance the growth of those two things through meditation, reflective self-inquiry, mindfulness and asking meaningful questions, and visualization." Olympic and professional athletes, both men and women, use visualization for increased attention, perception, planning, and body memory. It's been found that our imagination produces the same brain activity as the actions in the body. On our journey together, we are visualizing inspirational images to help rewire your brain for increased confidence, and to activate your inner warrioress potential. This is the power of a vision quest.

Always start by sitting in a quiet and comfortable position as you plant the desire and intention to find your unique magical talents of empowerment. Imagine that you are standing poised, strong, and invincible in front of a large pyramid made up of the materials and size of your choosing. The first image that pops into your mind is the correct image; simply trust the process of your visionary mind. Close your eyes at any time to find your images. Even if you don't see a pyramid at this point, your intuition is aware and open to receiving information from the collective Pyramid of Light.

Enter the pyramid in your mind's eye, and notice what specific semi-precious stones and crystals the walls and the floors are made of. What colors pop into your vision? Sometimes colors have very specific meanings for us; yellow, for instance, is the resonating color of the solar plexus, while gold maintains the energetic frequency of All That Is. Now imagine a great hallway with a large marble table in the center. You go to it and find an ancient tablet with your name on it. It is a tablet of recognition. The skills and talents you inherited in this lifetime are listed in bold archaic script. Added to this list are your potential superpowers that the warrior goddesses bequeathed you before your soul landed into your body. Take a look at the list of potential skills the warrior goddesses have suggested for you, and imagine using a colorful plumed writing instrument to add any talents your guides may have missed. Pause to add these words to your personal journal.

Many of us had to adopt patterns of behavior in order to survive or navigate the world around us. Just like our fears, shames, and pains, our energetic patterns have a light side to them. For example, I developed the superpower of invisibility so I could avoid any patriarchal outbursts within my family system. I can blend in, barely breathe, walk on air with silent steps, and I always know where the exits and hiding places are. This pattern evolved through fear, and I became unseen in the world. I had to learn how to use this skill to my advantage. Invisibility is neutral until you put a negative or positive label on it. Now I use invisibility to avoid distractions as I reflect, write, create, or need to focus on a project. I can use my invisibility gifts when I enter a crowded space and want to assess the patterns in the room before I engage with the crowd. Trust your gut as you write down your solar plexus superpowers.

When you are finished, see past the marble table and imagine a large staircase with golden handrails and jeweled lining leading up to a corridor high above the pyramid floor. There are seven beautiful rays of light streaming into this opening. You slowly make your way up the staircase until you arrive at the very top.

Allow yourself to pass through the intense rays of light directing you toward another hallway. At the end of this long passageway, you can see a closed door. It is a grand wooden door, heavy and heavily decorated with ornate carvings of a variety of warrior goddesses in action. Your heart quickens with the knowledge that when you enter the room, you are agreeing to their initiation process. It is a great responsibility to own your power and to use it only for good – let this sink in before you walk in. You look at the doorknob made of yellow sapphire and hold it in your hand before turning it to push the door open.

The room you enter is decorated with wall-to-wall gold leaf, almost blinding you with its brilliance. On the golden walls hang every weapon and useful artifact that you can imagine. Gilded swords and ornately-sculpted daggers populate one wall. An ancient Chinese crossbow and a South African assegai lay against a corner near metal-plated armor. Your eyes land on a Byzantine flamethrower and you are tempted to touch it. Every type of weaponry is here for you. At the far end of the room, you see the goddess Athena. She is stunning in her suit of armor, standing with ultimate authority and refinement. Athena explains that each of these weapons has a code of unique power, programmed with right action, truth, justice, and mercy. These weapons cannot destroy or kill a person, but they can destroy the negative energies, such as lies, betrayals, criticisms, and hatred, that a person can use as a weapon against you, or you against them. Look around. You may choose just two weapons. Choose wisely.

If you are having a hard time locating a weapon, or cannot decide on one, allow Athena to guide you to the most appropriate one for you now. There is no wrong answer or choice; it is the best weapon for you at this moment in time. Allow for the process to unfold and go to your journal whenever you need to write down any epiphanies. It is encouraged.

When you grab your two weapons, you exit another door from the golden weapons room and find yourself in another space where there is another goddess waiting for you. She is magnificent and wise and incredibly beautiful with wild golden hair surrounding her majestic face. She carries a large pointed arrow. You can see that she embodies a rare and unique light force. Heat emanates from her body and it looks like she has embers in her eyes. She seems to be made of solar fire. By her side is the animal that you saw in the jungle. This goddess beckons you to walk slowly toward her. When you meet, she offers you a generous and humble bow. This goddess tells you that she is going to share with you your strongest gift, your most potent magic, as she pets the animal beside her. She leans over and whispers into your ear with a sensual growl, "I am the protector of pharaohs, the healer of disease, the mistress of life. I am Sekhmet." She places both of her hands on your shoulders to straighten your posture. And with a quick motion, she pulls you into her body. In an instant, your childhood flashes before your eyes and you can see the wounded daughter, innocent victim, abandoned youth that you once may have been, in rapid transformation to become the most exquisite inspiring and empowering woman, grounded with Earth Empress energy, sensually in flow, creatively alive, and equipped with the eternal magic of death and rebirth. You become one with this Solar radiance, and stand up tall to feel the lioness goddess inside you.

This would be a great time to contemplate all the imagery and write down in your journal the images of what two weapons you carried and what your strongest gifts were.

Only when you have decided that it is a *must* to embody empowerment, not a *should,* does this cosmic fire begin to churn and burn and ignite the electric and magnetic field within your soul. At this stage, your power requires no permission from any teacher, authority figure, family member, friend, or book (including this one) because you realize that your power is your Truth. Power needs no explaining, offers no excuses, does not discriminate. Power is simply there, waiting to be plugged in to passion, purpose, and a desire so grand that the wisdom of your body simply unleashes it out into the Universe.

{Lesson: You have inner strength and a battalion
of Warrior Goddesses supporting you.}

Animal Magnetism

Magnetic. Mesmerizing. Electrifying. Unforgettable. Hypnotic. Attractive. Delightful. These are words to describe someone with a good dose of Animal Magnetism. Animal Magnetism is that unmistakable-yet-mysterious vitality that fascinates and attracts. It can ignite a little fear in you too, but it never repels. The term "mesmerizing" was first used to describe the hypnotic process that German physician Franz Anton Mesmer used to treat his patients. He called it Animal Magnetism. Mesmer assumed, as I do, that the invisible electromagnetic charge radiating from his body was channeled through the creative cosmic life-force energy. Animal Magnetism, then, is Kundalini serpent power, sex appeal, that very magical force that creates, gestates, and births life.

Let's be completely honest: this very yummy energy is attractive from the inside out. It is the fiery element that allows us to live with passion and purpose. A strong woman who possesses this light force energy is a dynamic and charismatic visionary leader who inspires others to be their best selves. In mutual friendship, this energy is the magnetic presence in the room that draws people in and the electric energy that animates and stimulates conversations. For intimate relationships, this dynamic energy offers polarity, tension, sexiness, vitality, and the creativity needed to keep a relationship alive.

Wild animals have this raw and potent magnetism. Humans are part of the animal kingdom, so we too are erotic creatures that naturally possess this energy. This kind of electromagnetic force is intimidating to those who fear true empowerment, which is why it has been criticized and bullied out of so many women. We can rekindle and refine this mesmerizing essence by integrating the natural instincts of our power animal. Power animals are equivalent energetic matches to our energetic soul signature. Everyone can have a power animal. Your family can have a power animal, as can your race etc. You don't often choose your power animal; your power animal chooses you. As mentioned before, we also have guide animals, which serve us as protectors, advisors, and helpers. They can be ocean animals that help us navigate our emotions, or show up to teach us something. They can be the primal animals that are either predators or prey to help us get back into the animal of our sensual bodies. Guide animals are usually our favorite animals, as they possess the traits we need at a specific time. We also have shadow guide animals, which are the animals we fear the most. They come to warn us when we are off track, or show us which shadows still need attending to. All of these untamed, free-spirited beautiful creatures teach us a great deal about ourselves.

We have always had an innate and deep relationship with animals, like our pets, that serve us on an emotional and spiritual level. Since humans became bipedal, we used the meat of animals to nourish our bodies, or borrowed their strength to help plow the fields. Energetically, all animals have symbolic meaning. The essence of the each animal exhibits another way the cosmos tries to communicate with and guide us. Right now would be a good time to be aware of your power animal.

To find your power animal and learn why its influence is so magnetic, we practice the Cosmic Law of Least Resistance. Bastet is the goddess we will invoke to personify this energy. She is a predator, and predators live this naturally. Bastet does not exert much energy until she needs to. A panther will wait for its food to come to it and use its powerful jaws and sharp claws to capture her meal; an eagle uses her large wings and keen eyesight to soar above the earth to find her prey below; the octopus changes colors to blend into her surroundings, and tentacles to feel every nuance; the hummingbird's unique wings allow her to fly backward, and hover over the flowers to retrieve their nectar with her straw-like tongue. I mention these magnificent animals because nature often teaches us how to be in the world instinctively and with ease. Your unique primordial, as well as cultivated, talents help you find and refine your divine purpose and understand how you love and how you want to be loved. This is felt through you and only you. Any outside referencing from friends, culture, family members, or gurus is not a true knowing. We get into the animal of our body to know our body, our instincts, our desires, our purpose, our meaning, our love.

When you are in resonance with your inner being, that place of infinite potential, your signature vibration adds variety and resonance with people in your life, to inspire and elevate passion and purpose for them too. This personal signature of yours is the reason for the dynamic and harmonious symphony of the world. Think about the jungle and the incredible sounds that the diverse creatures in the hidden wild create. It is extraordinary. While unveiling your unique power essence, the soul that matches your soul hears the call and is on their way to travel the journey of love and life with you. If you have ever wondered why a relationship isn't working, or why you are calling in the wrong type of person, it is because your resonance simply needs a little more clearing so that your call is not confusing. Your purely refined animal magnetism and primordial instincts will emerge when you stop resisting and start practicing the Law of Least Resistance.

The Law of Least Resistance is about living in the present moment. Not one second ago, or in a few seconds, but right *now*. Staying physically and energetically connected to the earth grounds us in our bodies. Self-awareness and the ability to name our feelings as they come up takes us home to the here and now. When we awaken to our unique rhythm and flow of life, we accept ourselves for who we truly are. The oak tree does not try to be a fish, nor does the wind try to be the earth. Each of us are powerful and necessary in our own ways. We experience authentic power when we take responsibility for our own actions, give up apologizing for ourselves, and no longer need to convince others to see our point of view. We get to this self-sovereignty by tapping into the primal energy of our power animal.

To find your power animal you will need to open up to the sacred animal world and ask them to come to you, through the powers of Bastet. Many women have an affinity for, or traits of, the feline species. Cats are sensuous, slinky, mysterious, powerful, and graceful. Cat guides are known for their healing abilities, agility, unpredictable nature, their detachment, grace, and ease. Since they have nine lives, they also represent the natural rhythm of death and rebirth. My numerologist describes the number nine as the energy of truth and authority. Those who can activate this champion-like energy have the desire to serve humanity through compassion and generosity. Their spirits ooze great solar power and unconditional love.

Nine symbolizes the ninth dimension, or that is what Bastet "told" me. Some of us are open to a field of energy higher than this third-dimensional planet. Empaths, telepaths, and mediums tap into this realm for their clairvoyance (seeing the invisible beyond), clairaudience (hearing messages as thought), or clairsentience (feeling messages as body sensations), or claircognizance (clear knowing). Ninth-dimensional entities can sense the feelings, emotions, and thoughts of others from a higher vantage point of no time or space, then they decide whether to communicate via spoken or unspoken languages to those who listen and can translate these messages properly. Cleansing and elevating the lower root, sacral, and solar plexus chakras to their highest function allows us to be clairsentient. We all have this ability and it is very useful when interacting with others to *feel* who is going to be a challenge or a support, to make choices that are best for our bodies, and to know who to intimately share our body and soul with. This is what "gnosis" means: knowing the magical, mysterious, primal, spiritual wisdom of the unknown.

During a few of my personal vision quests, I've seen Bastet shapeshift from woman to cat and back again. I take this to represent the very nature of feminine energy in flow. Our ability and necessity to shapeshift is important. We can shift like the wind, shape like the earth, flow like water, blaze like fire, and be still like space, while at the same time being true to our core essence, and that is the magic of relating in the material world as an eternal soul in a body.

Nine also happens to be the numerology of wisdom, initiation, and global consciousness. Whether or not you believe in such symbology, it doesn't hurt to curiously slink into the mysteries hidden in the most sacred spaces in our erotic bodies.

If you are ready to meet your mystical magical power animal, all you have to do is get yourself into a comfortable position and place your right hand on your solar plexus and your left hand on your belly. Breathe in naturally and normally. Relax your mind, allowing all your thoughts to dissolve into the ether to analyze another time. With your mind clear and empty, your forehead can relax and allow the skin around your eyes and temples to smooth out. Putting the tip of your tongue at the roof of your mouth where your gums meet your teeth helps to relax your jaw and connects the microcosmic orbit loop, the continuous flow of energy through your body as taught by Qi Gong and other martial arts. Try and relax your muscles so they fall off your bones from neck to toes. Invoke the image of the cat-like goddess Bastet. She is sensual, regal, beautiful, cunning, and mysterious. She can see in the dark.

Imagine that she is showing you the way through an enchanted forest or mysterious jungle, protected under the dense canopy of rich foliage. The sun filters through the incredible leaves lighting up a pathway before you. With your subtle sense of hearing, listen beyond the noise and confusion of this world and hear the rustle and motion of living breathing organisms of the earth and the crunching of the ground beneath your feet. Listen closely to the other sounds that pique your interest. Take a deep nourishing breath in, feel and smell the fresh mist in the air through your nostrils and into your lungs to connect your body with the presence of the trees. Look around to see what colors and images the jungle has to offer you. Are there butterflies or dragonflies near you? Are there any colorful flowers that make you gasp with awe and beauty? See with your subtle sense of clairvoyance what is beyond the deep jungle.

Envision a beautiful waterfall spilling into a large pond surrounded by majestic grass. You notice that there is a cave behind the waterfall; curiosity pulls you to enter it. You test the water and it is the perfect temperature for your body to swim in comfortably. Maybe you would like company? If so, ask your emotional sea guide to join you. As you swim easily and effortlessly like a mermaid or water nymph toward the waterfall, the air becomes thinner from the mist of the raging falls. Take a deep breath in and quickly swim through the powerful waterfall and into the quiet cave behind it. Your eyes and hearing are heightened now as you enter the black obsidian cave. Obsidian is a stone that has the powerful properties to purify any psychic pollution in your auric space, and it protects you from any negative energy.

At the far end of the cave you see an opening full of light that draws you to it. The closer you get to this point of radiance, you notice that it reveals a meadow of acceptance and truth that lies just beyond the lush jungle. There is no right or wrong here, just promising and liberating space. You walk out of the cave and onto a path. Continue walking slowly and deliberately until you see a clearing ahead of you. As you get closer to this meadow you see at a distance an animal. What is the animal that came into your vision? Is it standing or sitting? Note your feelings as you witness this exquisite primal creature, whose spirit resembles yours. When you think of this animal, turn to your journal and write down all the qualities of this animal, both good and bad, how they walk the earth (in herds or solo), their gifts, their challenges, and what you think is their most desirable trait. This is your power animal.

We add this primal energy to fuel your desires, whether it be material gain, peace of mind, and especially the love and passion you deserve in this lifetime. It creates the polarity, the friction, the juice of manifestation. As explained earlier, life does not exist without polarity. Nothing unmanifest will become manifest without this electromagnetic pulse. It is the necessary ingredient for creativity, life-force energy, attraction, lasting soul love, and, yes, phenomenal sex. Welcome to the jungle beauty.

*{Lesson: Animal magnetism attracts desires
with the least resistance.}*

Predator or Prey?

"It takes great courage to admit that you might be part lioness and part goddess, and even greater courage to love as fiercely and as gently."
—Lord Coltrane

In ancient matriarchal cultures, a woman's sexuality was her power *and* her pleasure. Sex, as you know by now, is one of humanity's greatest shadows, especially for women, as expressed by the stories of Eve, Lilith, and Magdalene. I purposely repeat that our sexuality is the very essence that creates all life, yet guilt and shame are infested with it. This diminishes the power of women. When we admit to the pleasure of it, a bigger shadow looms over us. We've been trained by society to revere suffering over feeling ecstatic, even though our bodies are organically meant to feel pleasure through our sensitive nerve endings. It is time to redefine pleasure as a way to connect, heal, become soul-aligned, and spiritually awakened to eliminate the shame and guilt we carry – so we can take back our power. Divine feminine sexuality elevates the superficial experience of body based pleasure to an exalted form of co-creation, where two souls connect as a portal into divine presence.

The profound injustice of patriarchal authority, privilege, and money are directly associated with the shadow side of power. Dominance, oppression, and manipulation are what keep a woman from owning and expressing her prowess. This is what keeps us in the faux feminine category. I believe that real power is never *over* someone, it is a source from within. Once we put our hardships through the renewal and alchemy process, this power can never be taken away. Authentic power is the awareness of your strengths and weaknesses. Authentic power is truth, clarity, humility, and grace. Authentic power is facing your fears, loving yourself as you move through fear and pain to the other side, and finding the pleasure in the process. Understanding that our sexuality and our animal magnetism are a source of power, and owning that power, is the only way we can never be overpowered or disempowered again.

As we've already discussed, polarity is the dynamic energetic exchange of opposite poles; the masculine and feminine, electric and magnetic, predator and prey *energies* that our primal bodies know instinctively. Learning to embody a healthy balance of both predator and prey energy is a skill. Balance and flow is essential to self-mastery, and polarity is essential to mastery with your relationships. Mastery of this erotic power is a skill worth cultivating.

To review, once our lower power centers are cleansed of fear, shame, and guilt, we add a little hunger and passion to the root chakra to stimulate the Kundalini energy that once lay dormant. When this energy awakens and flows into the sacral chakra, it activates the creative and sexual juice to energize your desires. When your sense of belonging in this world aligns with planetary consciousness and further aligns with your desire, they are elevated into the solar plexus, where they transform into purpose. Essentially, the karmic lessons you came into this human existence to master become your dharma – your soul's greatest purpose in this lifetime. Sexual energy embodied is your animal magnetism. The balancing of tension between masculine and feminine energy, or predator and prey energy, is absolutely key to maintaining balance in the world. And this electricity and creativity are what is required for romance and intimacy to thrive in your soul-centered relationships.

Intimacy is how deeply we can feel and express with another soul without inhibition. Trust and vulnerability are high vibrational states of being and a must for the awakened woman. Intimacy, at the highest and deepest level, is sharing a cosmic soul vibration with another cosmic soul vibration. Each time your flesh merges into the exuberant and passionate orgasmic abandon, another song of the soul is created. You will remember, for just a brief moment, what ecstasy feels like in the higher dimensions of surrendered infinite love.

That brings us to the fun part of this book: we get to use our erotic edge to cultivate the body memory of heavenly bliss. All living things are alive with eroticism. "Eroticism" simply means being energetically alive. It is an invitation to witness the blossoming of life. Just watch a lioness stalk her prey, or a rose blooming, both innate erotic expressions of natural movement. When you get rid of the "needy" energy that tries to fill up a hole inside you through the love of another person, or the drive of success that masks an insecurity of not being enough, then your energy becomes more exalted. This clear feeling of deliciousness settles into your body as your vibrational *yes* to choosing or knowing if something or someone is a match for you. At this stage of knowing, you begin to be your own oracle. You are the boss of you, and you should never forget that.

To break through the resistance of owning your own genius and quickly get to this blissful feeling, simply think of a lover or future lover and write down your sexual fantasies. As a reminder of the lessons of Lilith and Eve, our sexuality is our power, not something to be shamed. There is a lot of scientific research to suggest that sexual fantasies are normal products of the mind as she meanders through memories and experiences. Fantasies have proven to improve sex and promote more intimate romantic experiences. In a study conducted by Drs. David Ley, Justin Lehmiller, and sex advice columnist Dan Savage, sexual fantasies reflected individual personality needs. The cosmos has no judgment on our creative, curious, or sexual fantasies. Statues of antiquity, as well as the many Hindu and Buddhist deities, are depicted in the nude to represent liberation, raw truth, and purity of the *whole* self, including our erotic bodies. I'm sure they evoke a fantasy or two even from the most reverent among us. Elevating the soul does not mean we ignore the body. Lightning will not strike you down.

If you are still shy or embarrassed, even if no one will ever know what you are doing, just note that feeling without any judgment. Sometimes we have to go to unexpected places to break the bonds that keep us from feeling and knowing. Remember, no one is reading your mind. In fact, not even psychics can read your mind if you do not agree to it. The reason we write down your most hidden sexual fantasies from a place *without shame* is to distinguish between the yearning of your purely *physical* sexual needs and your *integrated* needs of the mind, body, heart, soul, and spirit. Going to your erotic edge is seeing more of your shadow from a place of empowerment and non-judgment, revealing where you need to go next as it fuels your soul's desires. All of the images and dreams conjured up in our minds are metaphors for unresolved experiences or those we want to explore. They do not necessarily mean you play them out sexually. For example, a dominatrix fantasy often relates to one's desire to be more powerful in the world or in one's relationship. It is our fantasies that allow us to play in the realm of make-believe so that we can try things out without any implications in the real world. With all that said, a sexual fantasy can be as simple as imagining the heat of the sun penetrating every inch of your bare skin.

Research on the benefits of joyful anticipation suggests that planning a future event gives us heightened emotions that feel better than the actual experience. Imagine planning a trip to Tahiti or another favorite place with your beloved. Think about the things you will do, the meals you will eat, and the adventures you will experience together. The joy in planning and envisioning is often more exciting because you aren't focusing on the mundane or challenging parts.

The heightened passion of tapping into your eroticism through fantasy is the feeling that helps manifest your desires more quickly. Because when you *feel* good, and are "tuned in, tapped in, *turned on*," to quote Esther Hicks and the Law of Attraction, your desires, or your project, or the energy you put behind your relationships, will gain momentum and excitement. Try adding a little predator and prey energy into the mix of your fantasy, or any creative pursuit. *Feel* the dominating energy in your body as your hunger, craving, or thirst and *see* your desires or your relationships as being the very thing that will satisfy that insatiable yearning for fulfillment. And then add a bit of *surrender*, softening, devotion, and sensuality to this idea. I'm using the predator and prey metaphors because they are the same energies that work in the cosmos. Electricity, magnetism, yielding, friction, explosions, and stillness are forces that flow with constant ecstatic motion in outer space and your inner space.

Use this very energy to inspire your words to write an erotic love letter to yourself, explaining every single thing you want to do or have done to you. After you are finished, read it to yourself so that your body has a memory of unbridled pleasure *without shame*. Know that you can burn it afterwards, or give it to your lover. Balancing these polar energies is how to flow in the world, but first you have to ignite them.

Aside from predator and prey energy making for an amazing sexual experience with your beloved, predation also teaches us about the cycles of life, death, and rebirth of creation; a theme that dissolves the rigidity of our fears, knowing that each moment we are growing and evolving is a natural state of being. Survival, hunger, and passion allow for you to focus on your goals, whether that be in romantic partnership, service in the world, or your next project. We learn to live fully in the present moment and learn our natural rhythms to flow with universal energy. We accept and know who we truly are, and we take responsibility for our own feelings and actions. No blame. No defensiveness. No need to try and convince others of our point of view. Just like the lioness who relaxes in a field until she is ready to feed her cubs, who can easily transition from ferocious to nurturing, the gift of understanding your unique ray of light is being who you are and knowing what you are made of without question.

{Lesson: Your erotic edge cultivates the body memory
of being alive with heavenly bliss.}

Holy Warrioress

If you haven't already guessed, I am guiding you on what I call a shapeshifter's journey. It is similar to what author and mythologist Joseph Campbell coined, the hero's journey, which explores the archetypal hero and heroines of myths and legends who transform their ordinary lives into extraordinary experiences. There aren't many female heroines depicted with almighty challenges to overcome, except for comic book superheroines like Wonder Woman or the deity myths of goddesses like Kuan Yin, Isis, and Lakshmi. Most stories of powerful women get cut short, like Lilith's and Eve's, and the prophet Magdalene being demoted to prostitute, to diminish the value of the conscious feminine.

You, sacred Warrioress, are on a shapeshifter's journey. Your legendary odyssey is within the depths of your *multidimensional* soul, where you find the allies and villains within yourself, *as yourself*, who test and reflect the wisdom, skills, and courage just waiting to be unleashed into the world. Joseph Campbell writes in his book *The Power of Myth*, "I think that what we're seeking is an experience of being alive, so that our life experiences on the purely physical plane will have resonances with our own innermost being and reality, so that we actually feel the rapture of being alive." The tales of the goddesses are metaphorical seeds planted into your psyche to mirror your inner adventures, which inspire the unfoldment of your greatest potential.

The meeting of the *many* facets of the self is when you feel the exquisite nature of your *whole* being. Now it is time to call in Holy

Warrioress energy to incarnate through us so that we can revitalize our inner resources and find our hidden strengths. Because we no longer have to worry about instinctual survival needs from predators, warring primeval clans, or being cast out of the group, our instinctual and Reactionary Responses have an opportunity to turn into a Reflective Response that works with our Earth Empress energy to have conscious reverence for this life-sustaining planet and every sentient living creature on it.

The Reflective Response is the ability to intercept fear based triggers with active listening, restful awareness, and the inspiration for right action. As we continue to reclaim and unshame the sexual and wild woman archetypes, invoke the energy of the Sacred Sexual High Priestess, and walk into the transformational fires to dissolve unnecessary fears, shames, and guilt that our inner victim, prostitute, or saboteur might still be holding onto, we exercise our Creative Response. We then recreate our stories and co-create with the cosmic powers that surround us. Our emotions no longer define who we are. We consciously know that our feelings are magical tools that unlock our sensitivities that link us with the energies of the goddesses who are living through us in many different ways. When you become the commander of various energies, each with their own unique polarity and influence, they can be directed to guide you toward your desires of love and purpose, as well as help pull in all the events and synchronicities for the fulfillment of your desires. Remember, epic love and soul purpose are your birthrights.

Now it is time to grow ourselves up and have that beautiful and tender innocent victim of yours, who may have adopted all of her patterns for survival, go through warrioress training. By understanding our patterns and then rewriting our life's stories, we transform them. Understand that the fear factors, such as anxiety and anger, are simply our fears unprocessed, anxiety being unprocessed fear that we continue to anticipate and expect, and anger being unprocessed fear that we continue to look back on and refuse to forgive.

As described earlier, everyone is made up of the five *mahabhutas*, or great elements of ether, air, fire, water, and earth. The ancient wisdom of Ayurveda teaches us that these primordial influences regulate our natural rhythms. The five elements are combined into three biological element categories called *doshas*. They are *Vata* (air and ether), *Pitta* (fire and water), and *Kapha* (earth and water). Although we have all of the elements in us, our bodies and minds do have two dominating *doshas*. Knowing them is helpful in all aspects of your life. In this context, we will discover your strengths and natural rhythms that influence your superpowers.

People with a predominant *Vata* (air and space) consistency tend to be naturally light and airy, joyful, always on the go, very creative, animated, lively, lean, and have an active mind. They have the quality of life-force energy. When imbalanced, they are forgetful, "air headed," or "space cadets," doing too many things at the same time, maybe even forgetting to eat. They might experience a challenge with the thought, *What did I do wrong?* The fictional character of Tinker Bell in the story of *Peter Pan*, created by J. M. Barrie, would be a good example of a *Vata* type. I also have a lot of Vata in me. Do you have the ability to shapeshift, flow with ease, and use your quick witted mind to creatively solve problems?

Those with a good amount of *Pitta* (fire and water) are intense and bright, direct, intelligent, confident, fiery, good leaders. They are athletically built, can eat anything, and have the quality of light force energy. When imbalanced, they might be aggressive, hot-tempered, prone to blame, argumentative. They might experience a challenge with the accusation, "what did you do wrong?" The feisty princess Merida from the Disney movie *Brave* is a good example of a *Pitta* type. This is my secondary *dosha*. Does your fiery nature help you get things done, and is your charismatic personality one that attracts and inspires others?

Finally, the *Kapha* types are strong, steady, grounded and loyal, and have great stamina. Their bodies tend to be solid and their actions slower. They are warm-hearted and reliable. They have the qualities of love force energy. When out of balance, a *Kapha* type can seem unmotivated, sluggish, or lethargic. Their stress response might be "I don't want to deal with what's going on." The character of Jessica Rabbit from the film *Who Framed Roger Rabbit* comes to mind for *Kapha*. I wish I had more *Kapha* to keep me grounded, I have to practice being rooted to the earth every day. Do you have the patience and capacity to love and nourish others for the long run?

An Ayurvedic practitioner can help you determine your dosha, but for now use your intuition to feel which qualities resonate with you best. Although it is beneficial and recommended to embody all the positive qualities of each element, let's focus on stimulating your fire essence.

The fire in your soul is a key to awakening your cosmic warrioress superpowers, and key to understanding the light and shadow aspect of this power center. When you read the description of fire, allow the words to come into your body as a felt sense. Fire is warm, it transforms, it lights up the darkness, it is radiant, it attracts. Saying the following mantras as affirmations will activate the positive fire qualities in your body. You can use them any time you need them. Say out loud, "I have the mastery of my energetic body." "I have the will to manifest all my desires." "I am the courageous and self-reliant lioness whose animal instincts are unparalleled." "I know my body's abilities and I am unashamed of my natural sex drive." "I am confident, magnetic, and have the incredible ability to empower others." "I am a leader of the love brigade, who inspires truth, breaks suffocating boundaries, and pioneers for the new world."

As you say each line, allow your body to receive your statements as truth. The more you use a mantra, it can turn into your personal *sutra*, or your string of aphorisms, collected and curated as your personalized sacred scripture. The energy behind your mantras, or affirmations, becomes infused in your auric field and energy boundaries. When the words begin to resonate and integrate as truth in your body, the world around you will reorganize to support your highest good.

I need to add a note of caution here. During the organizing process, some of the people around you will be triggered by your evolution. They will think you've changed and feel unsafe with this revelation of your truest nature. If you can learn to see the nature of their fear, it will help you to feel compassion for them. It is also necessary to note, again, that evolution is a natural rhythm of death and rebirth. All things are in a constant state of growing or dying, just at different rates. The essence of you, and everything and everyone for that matter, is the only thing that is eternal, loving, divine magic stardust. It is so hard for others to see it in themselves, so they will try to bully, shame, discredit, and humiliate it out of you. Your tools are your mantras, your continuous connection to the earth and her powers, your inherent talent as manifestor, Creatrix, transformer, the embodiment skills of the shapeshifter, and divine trust. You may have to let those that choose to stay in low vibration go, in order to make space for your soul family and soul love to enter. This is hard, but worth it. It takes great courage to admit that you might be part lioness and part goddess, and even greater courage to love as fiercely and as gently.

{Lesson: You are a fierce and powerful Shapeshifter
ready for anything.}

Love Avatar

Paradise Found

"And in the end, the love you take,
is equal to the love you make."
—The Beatles, "The End"

In just about every mythological story or fairytale there is a mystical garden oasis, or space where love, joy, beauty, peace, and abundance exist. These magical places are so poignant for us because they represent the purity and abundance of our hearts. Welcome to your true home beauties, welcome to paradise.

Paradise is found in the deepest chamber of your heart center, or *anahata* chakra. In this profoundly loving space, there is no loneliness, no lack, no fear, no shame, no guilt, no anger, no resentment. Our sensuality, our sexuality, and our spirituality are all equal here. You are the Creatrix of this space, and more than worthy of all it has to offer. What if a bounty of bliss, gratitude, forgiveness, grace, devotion, pleasure, and epic love were constantly swirling around you like a vortex? At the very core, we *are* this love energy. We *are* the source of all the love we experience, and all the love we give out. Many mystics and sages of sacred wisdom throughout history have claimed the same. The Beatles spent time in India on a spiritual journey before they released *Abbey Road*. Their final recorded lyrics sum it up: *"And in the end, the love you take, is equal to the love you make."* It is our souls' deepest desire to come back home to love, so that we can spread love unconditionally, share love intimately, and *be* love for ourselves and for those who need it. I am going to plagiarize my first book here, and simply repeat how I explain and see love.

Love is a verb. Love is the most divine action in the universe. Love cannot become a noun unless we stop searching for it and become Love (with a capital L) in the flesh. How we come back home to Love is by understanding what I call the Love Trinity. The Love Trinity consists of self-love, unconditional love, and intimate love. It helps us understand how to satiate our need for fulfillment, wholeness, *and* excitement. To consistently cycle through the three creates the high-vibrational rhythmic pulse of your heart. This beating connects all hearts, the heart of the earth, and the very Heart of this multiverse.

Self-love is honoring yourself on a physical, emotional, psychological, and intellectual level. It involves forgiveness and learning from our past (and maybe even past life) experiences. It is about knowing that *you* are more than enough, so *you* have overflowing amounts of love to share. Again, it is abundance mentality, it is inner beauty, it is inherent truth, it is self-empowerment. This love teaches us that the source of love is from within. This love is embodied.

Unconditional love is the love of all life, and all that life has to offer. It is the love of *All That Is*, it is Unity Consciousness. This kind of love exists at the physical, emotional, energetic, and astral planes. Through unconditional love you learn that you are always surrounded by love and have the power to heal through love. This love is spiritual.

Intimate love includes the flow and exchange of healthy passion, sex, connection, caring, admiration, deep emotions, and desires, *all at the same time*. It requires the mirror of relationships. Especially in intimate relationships, we see our own reflections, our deepest wounds, and our highest aspirations and potential. This love helps us to know the deep bonds of true intimacy, a union of our masculine and feminine energies, that reflect the sacred union of two souls. This love is soulfully mindful.

In order for us to feel fulfilled in love, we must integrate each part of the Love Trinity. Creating, calling in, and experiencing lasting sacred soulmate kind of love only happens when you love your *whole* self. It is impossible to love your whole self if you don't practice unconditional love. You can't test the resiliency of your self-love or your unconditional love without romantic love (even if this means you must have a love affair with your many selves first). This is why understanding the many personas within, asking the archetypal realms for guidance, and *becoming* Love (with a capital L) is so important. Love can always evolve in you, and resurrect in your current relationships. You can absolutely call in a lover and partner at the highest frequency and design your love together. You can, if you choose, experience the love for everything around you, and be one with All That Is.

Your paradise found is the embodiment of truth that you are Love in the flesh. This very moment is your opportunity to create a new world, a New Eden, where you are never alone. Here you will feel the bliss of eternal love and know that you are held and supported by the most magnificent and profound power whenever you need it. This of course requires trust and surrender to something so much bigger and more magical than you can ever imagine. When you get a felt sense of it in your body, you will never forget it. This is what the message of the High Priestess Magdalene has taught me, "your divinity is in your body."

Now would be a perfect time to introduce you to the Hindu goddess Lakshmi, who has been with me since birth. Lakshmi is known to be the goddess of love, beauty, abundance, and good fortune. All of these qualities placed in the heart serve others as kindness, inspiration, generosity, and grace. Even though I was not born with good fortune in terms of financial, physical, or emotional safety, I was always told I brought good luck to those around me. Lakshmi's story is a metaphor of my own, as she is a metaphor for many women on the path toward ascension.

I recall the tale shared with me at one of the many *satsangs,* or gatherings of enlightened souls, where I first heard the story of Lakshmi's resurrection and rebirth. The myth begins with her as the personification of Auspiciousness. She helped the warrior *deva* (minor god) Indra successfully protect the world from demons for many, many years. One day, Indra met an old sage sitting on the dirt road who offered the warrior deva a holy garland made of enchanted roses. Indra dismissed the gift and threw them on the ground with arrogance and disgust. In the legend shared with me, the old sage was Lakshmi in disguise, offering Indra even more opportunity for success. As you could imagine, Lakshmi was outraged by his vain insult and fled the world to obscure herself deep in the mysterious Milky Ocean.

Without Lakshmi's powers, the devas were no longer consecrated with her beauty, abundance, or good fortune. A shadow soon descended upon the world, and the devas began to lose their magical gifts. The people became greedy and shameful and irreverent to the deities. Demons began to take control over the world. Indra then asked the *bhagavan* (higher deity) Vishnu, who is also Lakshmi's divine consort, for help. Vishnu told Indra that he must churn the Milky Ocean over and over to conjure Lakshmi from her obscurity and regain her blessings to the world. Vishnu also shared with Indra that within the Milky Ocean was the *amrita,* the nectar of immortality, that would defeat the demons and allow the *devas* to live forever.

For years and years, the devas churned the Milky Ocean to no avail. With the world's tragic demise, both the devas and the demons had to collaborate. They began to churn the ocean together. Soon a poison came forth from the now-muddy waters that threatened to envelop the entire Universe. So they called on Shiva, the *mahadeity* – the Supreme Deity, the Deity of deities, the Almighty One – to swallow this poison. Shiva, as the masculine container that could hold this potentially dangerous alchemical liquid, knew he would not die swallowing the poisonous contents of the muddy waters for the resurrection of the goddess. He drank until Lakshmi was revealed unsullied and beautiful, sitting on a lotus flower with the elixir of life in her palm.

I share this story for many reasons. The first is to show the consistent metaphors of the divine feminine rising from the muddy swamp, or a cave, or an ocean of unknown, onto an exalted throne. Secondly, I would like to emphasize what the world would be like without the life-sustaining qualities of feminine energy: dark, grim, without beauty or hope. And finally, it is the merging of two sides, the shadow demons and the light devas, who had to unite in collaboration in order to resurrect Lakshmi. So many of us have risen from the depths of oblivion where our betrayals, shames, abuses, and vilifications once concealed the light. Like Lakshmi, we are being asked to churn our own oceans and dive deep into the unknown to know, to unite our shadow and light aspects to release the toxins of the lower vibrations, and rise unscathed and beautiful with the eternal powers to bring back life to this world. Your divine feminine love is so desperately needed on the planet now.

"The feminine is the most powerful dimension of life," says Sadhguru, "Without the feminine energy, or '*Shakti*,' there would be nothing in existence." Your heart center holds the immortal vision of your essence that has risen from shadows in your root center, mixed with the elixir of life-force energy from your sacral center. We alchemized any poison and tossed it into the transformational fire of your solar power, and then lifted it up into the heart center of Paradise. In other Hindu texts, Maha-Lakshmi, or the premier incarnation of the goddess, is also a personification of the Creator Goddess. The swampy roots of her lotus blossom represent the roots of all creation. To realize this goddess energy in you is to delight in the magic and artistry and lushness of life. To embody Lakshmi is to radiate your immortal soul out through your skin to inspire others with your loving light.

Before we integrate the powers of Lakshmi into our souls, I would like to mention Aphrodite, Mother Mary, and Sophia Christ to honor and awaken their unique energies already in your sacred heart. As you know, Aphrodite is the goddess of love, beauty, fertility, sexuality, and pleasure. We elevate her energy here in the heart center for the romantic qualities of the Love Trinity. Mother Mary has the qualities of the sacred womb, nurturing, and peace within. No matter what religion or spiritual practice resonates with you, Mother Mary is the persona and metaphor for unconditional, caring, and revered love for the self, before we bestow this love onto others. We integrate her energy as the self-love qualities of the Love Trinity. The Sophia Christ is the Judeo-Christian version of the Goddess of a Thousand Names and Faces, or The Great Cosmic Mother, similar to the varied and diverse traditions of Ancient Egypt's Isis, Shakti in India, and the Sumerian goddess Inanna. "*Sophia*" means "wisdom" in Greek, and refers to God's wisdom, or the feminine personification of the Holy Spirit.

I first came to know the Sophia Christ during the shamanic journey that I mentioned earlier. As Lady Gaia guided me to the Tree of Life and asked me if I wanted to know what the Tree of Life felt like, she was guiding me to Sophia. I had the visceral feeling that was unquestionably the embodiment of the divine feminine. This experience with Sophia Christ was one of love and wisdom like no other. I was one with the entire universe, and the universe was one in me. She gave me the insight to the reclamation of Eve and the return of Lilith to a New Eden, to the necessary rise of the divine feminine in you right now, and to the idea that the awakening of the divine feminine is what will resurrect the divine masculine. *The Nag Hammadi Scriptures* and the *Pistis Sophia* are ancient Christian and Gnostic texts that describe Sophia as a significant female deity. These sacred texts are the oldest we can find on Sophia Christ. I will be honest, going through these old texts is not an easy task for me, and it is the life work of many esoteric and religious scholars. I trust you will do your own homework if you find it interesting. For your reference, I recommend the copy of the *Nag Hammadi Scriptures* edited by Marvin Meyer, and the *Pistis Sophia* translated by G.R.S. Mead.

Sophia Christ in your heart, as the Great Mother, the feminine principle of God's wisdom, the Holy Spirit, the activated Sacred Feminine, is your unconditional love qualities of the Love Trinity. To integrate this in your heart chakra is to awaken to your most epic love story in all of eternity.

How to practice the embodiment of this Love Trinity is to first name it and claim it. You can continue to reprogram your nervous system by resisting the effort to control other people's opinions of you as your soul evolves, by living as the embodiment of the divine feminine, by responding to the signs the universe is trying to share with you, and by following your bliss.

Hold your right hand to your heart, and your left hand on your belly. Make sure that your energy is focused in the root chakra, or pelvic floor for grounding. When you feel grounded, focus on your sacral chakra to activate your empathic gifts before you bring your awareness up to your solar plexus to purify your energy even more. Then feel a swelling of love rise underneath your palm at your heart. Relax your body and pause to *feel* each statement as you say them out loud:

> "I call on the powers and guidance of Shakti, Sophia, Maha-Lakshmi, Mother Mary, and Aphrodite into my heart center and every cell of my being. I choose to embody the light and love wisdom of the Creator/Creatrix and All That Is. I claim the energies of the Divine Feminine. I embody the energies of the Divine Feminine. I take responsibility for my actions and service as the Divine Feminine. I am the incarnation of the Divine Feminine. So be it."

Integrate this as a body memory. The more and more you claim ownership of your divinity, and the more you have a felt sense of this divinity, you will receive the magnitude of your magic. Be fearless with this new sense of self, and witness the miracles unfold. It is not only right in front of you, it is and always has been inside you too.

{Lesson: Love is a verb that takes action in your heart.}

169

Resurrection of the Divine Masculine

"Dawn and resurrection are synonymous.
The reappearance of the light is the
same as the survival of the soul."
—Victor Hugo

As we learned in our rooted and wild discovery of Mother Earth, Eden is the abundant and all-loving primal earth that collapsed into the Garden of Good and Evil because of the shame of our spirituality, sexuality, and our inability to experience self-love. We took our fears and elevated them into the shadowy realms of our desire center to swim in the nectar of the goddess, and then lifted them further to transform into right action and empowerment. The earth, water, and fire qualities are now integrated as seeds of potential planted in the heart of paradise, your New Eden, your Heaven on Earth, your true home as the divine feminine.

You may have noticed that many of the major goddesses have sacred consorts that represent the divine masculine. We've already met Adam and Eve; their metaphorical energy exists in each of us, whether we are male or female. We already understand that they once lived in a pure loving paradise. Their fall into right and wrong and judgment separated them from Oneness. Shiva is the consort of Shakti. Shiva is the essence of pure consciousness, while Shakti is the dynamic and creative life force. This sacred couple represents the two essential aspects of the One: the masculine principle and the feminine principle. Other examples of the sacred union between masculine and feminine energies are Isis and Osiris, Lakshmi and Vishnu, Jesus and Magdalene, Kuan Yin and Babaji, Ascended Master Saint Germain and Lady Portia.

Energetically, we hold both the masculine and the feminine essence in our bodies. This is the yin and yang concept. The masculine parts of us hold space, protect, and plant seeds of potential, while our feminine essence nurtures, enlivens, creates, flows. Mastering a healthy balance of both masculine and feminine energy is important because we don't want to lose either when integrating the archetypes or while in relationship with another. The basic rooted masculine and feminine energy is also the foundation for the easy shift and flow through the varied vibrations of the other archetypes, like the warrioress, the goddess, and the sovereign. For practical material world experiences, we use warrioress energy for athletic competitions, goddess energy for weddings and other socially important events, and sovereign energy in our homes or as leaders in organizations. Understanding how we are rooted to the earth is also how we become grounded in our own bodies.

The biological-based male and the biological-based female naturally conduct energy differently. When we understand the polarity of both energies in our own bodies, we can conduct the energy consciously to better understand the energetic language between the sexes. If we aren't rooted in our biological energy and balanced within, we will look for energy outside of us to complete or balance us. That is why fully activating your inner divine feminine energies to resurrect your inner divine masculine energy is important. When we unite the two in sacred union for our own fulfillment and become whole, we no longer experience the neediness of relationships. This type of sacred union is the co-creation of growth and love together. Now it's time to meet your inner lover, the perfect masculine *energy* you have been searching for your whole life.

In this next transmission, we are going to imagine Lakshmi as our guide back into the heart of Eden with you as an initiated woman. The ravishing surroundings are familiar to you, only brighter and richer to your senses. It feels really good here, and it smells delicious too. Again, trust the process, and the imagery will evolve. You understand that you can create anything just through your thoughts here. If you are hungry, fruit falls off the trees for you. If you are thirsty, the river calls to you, allowing you to drink from her. Lakshmi leads you to a pool of deep dark water, that looks like the Milky Way galaxy with its inky black background and tiny shimmering lights dancing on the surface. Lakshmi asks you to look in the pool to see your reflection. This is your current inner woman. Close your eyes whenever you need more time to conjure up the image of your inner woman. What does she look like? Find the traits that characterize her, like her age, her dress, her posture. Once you are finished observing your inner self, Lakshmi takes you to a bridge that crosses a deep chasm. In front of the bridge are both Mother Mary and Aphrodite. They bestow you with their gifts of healing, caring, nurturing, love, beauty, grace, sensuality, and sexuality. Lakshmi offers you a garland of pink roses. Above them is the shimmering rose gold essence of Sophia, who infuses your body with bliss and pleasure and a warmth that feels like a loving embrace. She whispers to you, "when you heal the inner boy, you will reveal the divine man."

When you are ready, you are asked to cross the bridge to the other side, where a winged horse is waiting for you. You walk steadily and carefully across the bridge high above a dark gorge below. Once you cross the bridge successfully, you mount the winged horse and it takes you up into the sky, back in time, to a medieval castle on a hill. You walk up to this magnificent castle and step inside. Sitting in the castle is a young, troubled, and lonely boy. Take a look at this boy and notice what age he is, what he is wearing, and note his demeanor. You can see into his future, and know his blocks and his worries. He looks at you with a smile, relieved that someone has finally come for him. Depending on his age, you appropriately allow him to sit on your lap. You notice that he is sad and crying, so you offer him the unconditional and nurturing love you learned from Mother Mary, and you notice that he is growing in size and age. The more and more love you give him unconditionally, the more he grows and becomes stronger. Soon he becomes an adult man, sexually alive, and steps back from your coherent field of untethered love. He feels free, independent, cared for, honored, and adored.

When you feel his maturity and his readiness, you can infuse Aphrodite's balanced and fine-tuned sexual energy throughout your body. This charged energy is sent from your pelvic area to open his heart. He templates this safe energy from your body, and you can feel the opening of his heart and the flow of equal energy between you. He stands before you waiting. What age, demeanor, clothing, and other details are important now? The sound of Sophia's love wisdom asks if you are ready to unite in Sacred Union. Be honest. Are you ready to unite with your inner masculine? Is he mature enough? Is he healed enough? If you aren't ready to marry yourself, then there is more work to do to cleanse out the toxic masculine energies from your past experiences and from society at large.

On another vision quest, I was given the opportunity to feel how painful it is for the patriarchal masculine to separate his ego from his heart's intelligence. The toxic male is a little boy still, playing a man. He does not trust love or truly feel like he deserves unconditional or spiritual love, so he vehemently rejects it from the feminine divine who embodies unconditional love. More than his fear of the creation powers of the feminine, is his fear of being rejected and abandoned by her. This collective wound has plagued the masculine for millennia. The masculine's fear of abandonment turns into rage, then turns into power and control over the feminine. We need to love the immature masculine back into manhood.

The elevated masculine energy, or yang, within us are the solar powers we cultivate in the solar plexus. It shows up as external, active, penetrating, analytical, linear, strong, science-based, and thinking. Toxic, or immature, masculinity is aggressive, dominating, attacking, and narcissistic. You know by now, that the yin, or feminine energies, are internal, calm, receiving, creative, circular, soft, spiritual, intuitive, and feeling. The toxic, or faux, feminine is manipulative, jealous, defensive, passive-aggressive, self-loathing.

Organically, biological-based women penetrate *electric* energy with their heart centers, while biological males receive energy through the *magnetic* center in their hearts. Biological-based men penetrate electricity with their sacral center, while a woman's sacral center is the magnetic force that receives his energy. The need for the constant flow of energy can be understood by the Cosmic Law of Giving and Receiving. Everything in the cosmos is in a dynamic exchange of energy. Unfortunately, most men keep their heart centers closed to the feminine penetrating heart energy, while most women are closed to the penetrating life-force energy from the masculine. It is this closure of the loop of energetic exchange that keeps some relationships from experiencing ease and flow, adding to the misunderstanding of the sexes.

Learning how to awaken to an abundant, forgiving, grateful, life-sustaining essence of the feminine is the first step to integration of the whole. From this place, you resurrect the masculine energy within your soul. As an evolved, conscious, balanced, whole, loving creature, you attract the soul connections you crave. When there is a critical mass of ascended souls who love and heal at the highest vibration, together we help resurrect the entire planet. Sophia gifted me the image of self-anointed light brigade souls all rooted to the center of the earth. As we collectively ascended in vibration and pulled on the center of the earth's core together, a brand new earth burst forth. Love is ultimately your feminine genius, and it has the power to resurrect. Let's continue to cultivate it.

{*Lesson: The balance of inner masculine and feminine energies will attract the love you crave.*}

Divine Union

"It is not the merging of flesh, but the
merging of divine feminine and divine
masculine energies within your soul that
creates wholeness. You become a beacon
of numinous light that calls in the
sacred Other. From here you can dance
life together with awe and rapture"
—Lord Coltrane

As you have well received by now, I have been streaming a few downloads from the Masters of Love that live in dimensions beyond this three-dimensional world. I know it is my purpose to share this love wisdom to support the activation of your superpowers, so that you deeply feel that you are the ultimate goddess embodied. I do this through revealing the relationship of your multifaceted self and coaching you to fall madly in love with yourself, so much so that you feel blissfully whole. This is sacred union. The benefit of sacred union within your soul first, is that you get to experience this kind of divine love with another. As above, so below. As within, so without.

We will have an opportunity to come together in sacred matrimony, but first let me explain a little bit about the three dimensions of love. I know it is difficult to conceptualize the flow between unity consciousness and the definitions that make us individuals, but this is the dance of the divine: holding the tension between all worlds, as one world, in easy and graceful flow. Thank you for surrendering to the mystical mystery that is cosmic rapture.

The three dimensions of love are found in the differences between karmic lovers, soulmate lovers, twin soul lovers. All are mirrors of relationships, depending on what you came to this planet to do and learn. These are labels not set in stone, it is the energy behind them that matters. There is not one kind of love dimension that is better or worse than another, it is simply the vibration and intention you hold in your body. I am sure there are plenty more dimensions of love out there than we humans can comprehend. But for now, feel into your body to know what vibration your love dimension is currently in. Again, there is absolutely no right or wrong here.

Karmic love is essential and exceptional, and is the type of relationship most of us on this planet experience. You are drawn to each other, feel comfortable with each other, and you might feel like destiny has brought you together for a reason. There are life lessons to be learned in this type of relationship, as if an invisible contract was formed before you came together on the planet to find each other and to re-experience your past life memories for your soul's growth. Because Mother Earth is a learning planet, our souls will call in the people and the experiences that we need to learn from in this lifetime in order to evolve.

At a basic level, some of us simply need to understand how to love by feeling safe in relationships, by understanding the currency of giving and receiving, by knowing our desires through and with others, by committing to something other than ourselves, and by feeling the erotic life-force energy that intimacy brings. At the third-dimensional level that is this earth plane, some of us struggle with commitment, trust, safety, and self-worth. Our relationships can be trying at this level because we are tested by betrayals, boundary issues, addictions, shutting down, emptiness, control, or smothering. From a higher standpoint, these are the greater experiences that challenge us to look deeper into our souls, to know ourselves better. For some, the renewal of a commitment, the forgiveness of a betrayal, and the journey toward embodiment and fulfillment are enough.

Your relationships can thrive after learning at this three-dimensional level. If this is your place, I recommend you fully enjoy the process of loving and learning. "Issues" can be dealt with smoothly when we understand what we can improve on and *choose* to improve on these things. If your karmic relationship has changed for the better, yours is a relationship of forgiveness and celebration that can influence many. For others, your soul might be asking you to awaken even further, and you might feel the yearning for more. If so, you are being asked to jump, headfirst, into the rabbit hole to search for a wholeness and spirituality that your soul is now craving. It is the feeling that asks, "Is this really all there is?" The answer is no, there is *so much more*! And that is why you are reading this book. You can soul search with a karmic lover. They can support you, eventually awaken too, or sometimes it means the end of the relationship.

Soul love is a different type of learning. Here is where you understand that we are souls in bodies, and bodies that are home to our souls. It is an "and not or" type of thing. "Woo woo" people who came into the world loving everybody without condition are soul lover types. They can call in soulmates who love unconditionally *and* intimately, with wild abandon. At this higher dimension of knowing, say the fourth and fifth dimension of the cosmos, you start to recognize your soul families – the friends, family members, teachers, students who are really and truly supportive of your growth and well-being, *without any personal agenda*. There is a natural give-and-take energy, sprinkled with gratitude. They help us explore the depth and breadth of our collective souls, and help us expand into and absorb the magnitude of spirit. Soul love relationships are typically aligned, inspiring, in flow, and the sex can be incredibly healing, inspiring, and erotic. Shame of sexuality is usually non-existent.

A soulmate is a uniquely special bond also felt through lifetimes. There is a sense of equality, harmony, destiny, and a growth connection together, versus the individual learning of a karmic relationship. Your energies are complementary. There can still be challenges between soulmates and soul love relationships (we are human!), but these challenges are met together without blame. It is the feeling that the two of you can conquer any obstacle together. This is a truly beautiful type of relationship, which can be intense, or soothing, or both! You encourage each other to be your best selves. Lucky you, if you are in this place. Enjoy! Yours is a relationship of inspiration and evolution.

Twin soul love has reentered the collective consciousness because of humanity's deep desire for a new paradigm of love and healing on this planet, and for this planet. It is a new concept to many, but it is the same idea as Shiva-Shakti, and God-Goddess, Creator-Creatrix, two aspects of a whole. Many soul seekers have their own definition of twin soul energy, so this is your opportunity to practice your gnosis and feel into what is correct for *you*. To understand it requires a little bit of detachment from the outcome, because it is meant to trigger ascension and the cleansing of the soul to remember divinity. This kind of love is a very rare and complicated love that has a greater purpose than the individuals involved. When reunited, twin souls are intended to amplify love and consciousness on this planet.

We can go back to the metaphor of Adam and Eve as being the split of Consciousness, the One, All That Is, by wanting to experience itself. That thought, or logos, sometimes referred to as the title Christ, was the impetus to learn through the wisdom, or Sophia, of experience. To paraphrase, Adam became the linear masculine, while Eve became the wisdom seeker, and they have been trying to go back home to Eden to find unity ever since. Twin soul love is the sacred union of two souls that are actually one. It is the ancient feeling of finally coming home to yourself, and then serving the planet through this type of love. This is devotional and in service to a much higher commitment.

If you have a twin soul on this planet (sometimes they do not incarnate at the same time), you *will* meet and your meeting will seem random at first. When your paths do cross, the bond will be intense and immediate. Give it time, for when you look back at your situation, all will seem perfectly orchestrated. That is the consistent account of the twin souls' rite of passage. To amplify love and raise consciousness on the planet is a lofty goal of ascension that only a few souls have agreed to do.

Twin souls are initiated for ascension, but split in two. These souls, now existing in two different bodies, have experienced many lifetimes separately to learn as much as they can before coming back together. Although many have yet to awaken to the truth of their destiny, these souls have chosen to come on this planet for a reason – to find each other and remember their divine purpose. The twin soul journey can be a challenging experience because one person is usually further along the process of awakening than the other. The one further along might need to help the other awaken and support the awakening. They also mirror for each other the healing of wounds that must happen before the soul can ascend, so personal issues like self-love, self-worth, self-trust, and knowing the Divinity within come up to haunt us into deeper healing. When twin souls finally get to reunite, it is two whole beings, fully human and fully divine, in sacred union walking the path of Heaven on Earth. On a basic level, Twin Flames experience bliss, joy, abundance, cosmic rapture, and erotic fire just by holding hands. The love and energy are so great that their very togetherness ignites the souls of others...and so the ascension of the human spirit begins to amplify and raise consciousness to a higher level. If you are a twin and found your flame, dig deep into your knowing and understand how rare and profound your work is on this planet.

When you awaken to Love Consciousness, you will rejoice in whichever dimension your soul chose to live and learn from. Your opportunity is to continue to discover how you love and want to be loved in this lifetime, and at this very moment.

{*Lesson: Sacred Union is the love between you and you.*
All dimensions of love build from there.}

Lost in the Hall of Mirrors

"Nothing ever goes away until it
has taught us what we need to know."
—Pema Chödrön

Our first relationships are never about our relationships, they are about teaching us who we are and what we have come here to learn, and thus inspiring our purpose in serving in our unique way. Relationships are reflections for us to see and know ourselves more clearly, especially in our intimate relationships. If we can learn from them, our relationships can grow to the next level, or we can transition out of them. It *does* take two people to keep the relationship growing. The adage "if you are not growing you are dying" is a law of nature.

On another one of my experiences beyond the veil of this material world, the Divine took me to the world between the worlds, where I decided the details of my life's story just before I entered this earth plane. I was taken on a winged horse all the way up to the heavenly fifth dimension. The Great Cosmic Mother gave me the imagery and body memory of a discussion with two very distinguished and honorable male figures. They would be significant teachers for me in this lifetime. They asked if I was sure that I wanted to learn these lessons through them. I felt like an inquisitive and eager soul excited by the opportunity. The two men were my father, and the man I married.

It is a very profound experience when you understand that you are the Creatrix of your own story. My father came into his lifetime as an abused, abandoned, and impoverished man who had to survive a war. He had a great deal of PTSD, so when he married my mother and the stress got too great, his unprocessed fears turned into neglect, uncontrollable rage, abuse, and threats with a gun. He gambled away money so my mom had to work two jobs, and he abandoned us for another family. Yet, he was also very charming, loving, and fun, it was very confusing. I feared my father for a very long time, and thought that all fathers were like him. My coping method was to go into my imagination, become invisible, and endure. I tucked that experience away as fast as I could, not knowing that I had my own set of PTSD symptoms because of it. I remember thinking that the one thing that hurt me the most was the idea that he left us for another family. For some reason, the abuse was veiled as us doing something wrong, and the gambling and money issues were just an external stress, but his affair made me feel like my very being was wrong and unwanted, like I wasn't good enough to keep him around. I felt responsible for him leaving.

When I met the man I was to marry, he was so very different from my father. I believed I was partnering with someone who could do no wrong. It wasn't much of a high bar, but I trusted his integrity to my core. He was definitely not like my father, but after seventeen years of marriage, I found out about his infidelity. The dam broke loose and all my childhood wounds came up to the surface to engulf me like the poison in Lakshmi's Milky Ocean. It was much more complicated than this, but I mention these two relationships because I unconsciously adopted victim mentality as I felt they were acting out against me. But when I started to trust my spiritual awakening and allow myself to receive guided information, I realized that these events happened *for* me to learn and grow. In this lifetime, I wanted to test my resilience and my faith. I wanted to go through a dark night of the soul (which happened a few times) so that I could unleash my feminine superpowers and awaken the goddess within. I wanted to know the nitty-gritty of relationships, I wanted to know my divinity, I wanted to learn epic love. These two relationships mirrored to me what my soul deeply wanted. I am so grateful for them.

What I have come to learn is that ancient Buddhist and Vedic wisdom, the teachings of the Gnostics Gospels, and other esoteric theologies express the same thing about consciousness, love, and relationships, just with different metaphors. As I understand from the Vedic tradition, unity consciousness is Oneness, meaning we are all reflections of each other to learn and experience and grow.

We will unconsciously seek out partners and relationships to help us master what our souls want to learn in this lifetime. I chose a father who would challenge my worth, and a partner who would help me refine the lessons of betrayal and self-sovereignty. Our difficult relationships are mirrors of the very shadows we want to bring to life. From a much higher vantage point, these souls love us so much that they were willing to serve us in this way.

Much later, I learned from author, scientist, and soul pioneer Gregg Braden about the Seven Mirrors of Relationships written in the Dead Sea Scrolls by the ancient Essenes. I admire him for his intellectual mind, his spirituality, and the research he does on the topics he shares. This information comes from my notes and memory during one of his live workshops, infused with my own interpretations. He writes about them in his book, *The Divine Matrix* and *Walking Between the Worlds*. "Whether they are conscious of it or not, every human will experience the presence of others, mirrors of themselves in that moment," he says regarding the Seven Mirrors from the Essene point of view. As you read the descriptions, reflect back on your significant relationship to determine your mirrors.

In my own words, the first mirror is labeled as a reflection of our pain and anger in the moment. These are the immediate triggers or reactions that generate the stress patterns of fight or flight. Unprocessed fears that turn into anxiety or anger that another person triggers in us are mirroring back the very forgotten or repressed pains in the rooted center that our souls want to transcend. This mirror is intended to wake us up, at least that was my experience as a child.

The second mirror of judgment is the reflection of our hidden and forbidden shame and guilt found in the sacral chakra that cause us to judge outwardly or inwardly. When we feel we are being judged, we can reflect on if we judge others, or if we judge ourselves. Of course, it is our choice to reject or accept these as reflections of disclaiming our shadow side.

The third mirror is a loss, as either something given away or taken away. I see this mirror as a reflection of our loss of potential in the solar plexus chakra. Loss dims the light of our fire, and we lose hope for ourselves. We will usually try to find the qualities we think we've lost or given away, and admire them in others. Sometimes you will put people on pedestals, or feel imposter syndrome when pretending to be something that is not yet fully recognized in you. When you project the qualities onto others that you admire, they are mirrors for your own lost desires and purpose.

The fourth mirror refers to our first experience of unrequited love in a relationship or lifestyle. The unconscious lover qualities are the traits of the inner prostitute who gives up her soul in desperation to feel connected, or the saboteur who gets in her own way of true loving partnerships. Manipulation, control, and power as money or sex might be the reflections back from false lovers who mirror back our lack of love for ourselves in the heart chakra.

The fifth mirror is said to reflect back to us our parental images. It is very common for people to find relationships to mimic the unresolved conflicts found through their parents' relationships. If one of your parents was absent, you might call in a partner who is also absent just so you could demand the presence that you craved as a child. Parents are such a great influence that we usually adopt their beliefs. The throat chakra is where we can tap into our authentic voice to be heard as an individual and speak our own truth. It is also the opportunity to set boundaries.

The sixth mirror is the reflection of the dark night of the soul. I have already described this as the shapeshifter's journey, where we travel into the abyss of the shadows to challenge our own demons. This is a spiritual quest to know the self. These reflections come from the people who offer us our biggest challenges and experiences. They can be parents or lovers, but it is the specific experiences that require us to ascend that test of the spirit and find the light. In the third eye chakra, we learn to see beyond the veil to the truth of our cosmic journey through life and see wholeness in separation, conflict through harmony, and witness the colorful prism at the center of shadow and light. This mirror reflects our soul's journey.

The seventh mirror reflects back our true self. I call this self-sovereignty. The relationships that we experience show us how we perceive ourselves. If we feel like a victim, we will call in people who remind us of that. If we are trying to lead in the world, but do not own our sovereignty, then we will find resistance from the people who challenge the very core of who we are. The crown chakra is where we finally integrate all of the many selves into this powerful wholeness to mirror back our divineness.

Essentially, through your relationships you can get lost in the hall of mirrors, or learn to see through the illusion and love what is mirroring back at you. All that surrounds you is a reflection of your inner being. When you claim all parts of you as divine, your relationships begin to change to reflect who you really are. When you smash the mirrors and turn your gaze inward to look at yourself, the mirrors turn into diamonds. As a diamond, you will shine bright with love.

{*Lesson: Be grateful for all your relationships.*
You chose them to serve your highest self.}

Love Avatar

"Lovers don't finally meet somewhere,
they're in each other all along."
—Rumi

It's time to integrate everything we've accessed so far with the expansive energy of the heart. Take a very big deep breath into your heart center and think about someone or something or some place that you love so much you can't stand it. Maybe even smile from the inside out with this scrumptious feeling. Tap your fingers on your heart to bring attention to that space, and allow your magical mind to create more richness, color, and texture to the imaginary journey we've already experienced. We are going to meet your divine counterpart once again through this next transmission.

When we elevate the primal man and primal woman back into the heart space of Paradise Found, we reclaim our true heritage and birthright as sacred sexual, creative, empowered beings infused with divine love. Here, we embody all nature's elemental qualities to expose your heart's radiance. Your New Eden is securely grounded to the center of the abundant and generous earth, allowing you to be rooted and wild. As the earth, you can be as majestic as the highest mountain and hold yourself and others as Earth Empress. You will exude nourishing energy to heal, feed, and care for your loved ones as earth's sacred plants do. Here, you flow like the sensual river meandering through life, giving and receiving, finding life delicious and pleasurable. You are deep, mysterious, and sensitive as the ocean's emotional intelligence merges with your own. You are calming and tranquil like a pond. The fire in your heart blazes with fierce love, twinkles with inspiration, and flickers with seductive tenderness. Like air, you shift and change, you are the breath of life that caresses others with your gentle touch. And like the cosmos, you are the empty vessel of infinite possibilities, the impulse of creation, and the dynamic everything.

The awakening of the divine feminine within is the key to resurrecting your inner divine masculine. Uniting the two in sacred matrimony is the completeness of the yin-yang circle, the eternal heartbeat of the Universe as Shiva-Shakti, the perfection of God-Goddess, the holiness of your whole being. When the two polar energies are united, we are complete. We are the abundant self, instead of the limited self. There is a freedom and happiness in the heart when you no longer need anyone to validate you. Your future relationships will not exist to fill a gap, or taunt you into pivotal triggers, or catapult you into the abyss of the unknown. Your new soulful relationships will exist so that you create and inspire and grow together as a conscious whole, in whatever dimension you choose to love in.

This is the crucial moment when you get to choose. "You must give up the life you planned in order to have the life that is waiting for you," says Joseph Campbell. Will you choose old habitual patterns of relating to yourself and others, or are you ready to give that all up and become a Love Avatar? You, as Love Avatar, love with the highest integrity without giving up yourself. You communicate love with authentic expression. You are so inspired by love that you embody a feeling that is more than butterflies, but a kind of rolling thunder inside your belly, ready to explode. Your love is both a fierce energy and the softest of kisses. Are you ready for a madness that can hardly be contained when that soul that you've been searching for is no longer a dream?

Let's go back to your inner masculine now. Close your eyes to remember their face and their build and their demeanor. Are they ready, are you ready, to join in sacred matrimony? Imagine your beloved however you would like to see them. This masculine energy is the container that holds the flow of your feminine energy. You find balance and equality. Allow this relationship to transport you to another dimension where only love exists. All you have for each other at this moment is gratitude for finding each other. You hear the poet Rumi whispering, "Lovers don't finally meet somewhere, they're in each other all along," and you completely understand this message.

Imagine you are in a beautiful temple in Eden, surrounded by your heart's every desire. The high ceilings are extraordinarily lit up by thousands of candles on every surface, save for the path to the altar. On the altar are the emblems that represent a promise you made to yourself in the world between the worlds that hold you and you together in eternal union. Notice all the earth's elements decorating the altar, along with your weapons of truth. Everything you have ever cherished is represented on this altar. You have willingly given up everything so that you are empty and ready to receive the sacrament of divine grace. If you feel any resistance, your guides are there to help you along.

Imagine yourself giving up everything else that means anything to you, and releasing them to the altar. Your guide, soul, and power animals take away your primal magic, Lilith takes away your wildness and your freedom, Eve takes your shame and your curiosity,

Magdalene takes your guilt and your sensuality, Mother Mary takes your unworthiness and your love, Isis takes away your power and your light, Durga and Athena take your safety and your protection, Kali takes your rage and your righteousness, Venus and Aphrodite take your connection and your flow. Lakshmi takes away everything else. The ever-rotating essence of Sophia, Shakti, and the Great Mother Goddess is ready to take your life.

You are not afraid, for you know that once you are willing to give up everything to become the necessary emptiness of no-thing, this is when everything is spontaneously given to you. Be brave now, beloved. Release everything to be empty now. Feel the emptiness.

The universal vibration of OM is heard with the songs of Tibetan bowls and fills your empty vessel. As pure essence, you take the hand of your divine masculine's pure essence and walk up the aisle where the glistening golden stardust the Goddess of All Things waits to consecrate your union.

Her prayer and blessing to you is, "I AM, God-Goddess, Mother-Father, Shiva-Shakti, Source of All That Is, the Omnipotent, Omniscient, Omnipresent OM. You are the embodiment of the I AM, God-Goddess, Mother-Father, Shiva-Shakti, Source of All That Is, the Omnipotent, Omniscient, Omnipresent OM. We initiate you into the mystery school of Life and Love and Light. We bestow upon you the Holy Grail to be placed in your eternal sacred heart to overflow with the sacred nectar of the Goddess. You are restored to the beauty of ever-renewing truth of All That Is. You are Holy to receive the very essence of Divine Love."

Your feminine essence faces your masculine essence and you say out loud in unison, "I am the embodiment of the I AM, God-Goddess, Mother-Father, Shiva-Shakti, Source of All That Is, the Omnipotent, Omniscient, Omnipresent OM. I receive and accept the responsibilities of this Truth. The chalice in my heart is forever filled with divine grace, and I resurrect in wholeness as Divine Love. So Be It." Say this out loud three times so the Universe and everything in it hears this vibrational declaration.

In ritual ceremony, you come together with a kiss to anoint your blessings and merge as one. The reason why the collective consciousness is focusing on the rise of the Divine Feminine, and why I focus on it in this book, is because the qualities of the feminine are how we receive the Love Wisdom from the higher dimensions. We need to empty ourselves of expectations and surrender this wisdom. The power of the feminine resurrects the masculine. The genius of the feminine is in her humble knowing that both energies need to be equally integrated and stay in a continuous flow of giving and receiving. Our constant challenge as humans is to hold the tension of duality as Oneness.

Rest now, digest this transmission, and allow its nutrients to nourish your whole body. Give yourself permission to take a break from all you thought you knew about yourself. Imagine where you would go and what you would do on a honeymoon with your unified self. Adore yourself, admire yourself, love yourself as newlyweds do. Dream the dream of lovemaking and get impregnated with new desires, new creations, a new purpose, and the seed of pure potential waiting to be birthed in this new world.

And then hear the whispers of the universe to guide you even further...

{*Lesson: The first person who you should marry is yourself.*
Congratulations, by the way.}

CHAPTER 8
Cosmic Creatrix

Kiss of the Cosmic Breath
The Cosmic Mind
Song of the Soul
Cosmic Creatrix

Kiss of the Cosmic Breath

"If I breathe you in and you breathe me
out, I swear we can breathe forever."
—Iain Thomas

Lifetime after lifetime, we are asked to re-member, to re-learn, to re-connect, to know that something is whispering to us, charming us, blowing in our ears the miraculous primordial sounds of the Universe: a baby's cooing, a kitten's purr, the sound of the wind rustling in the leaves, your lover's breath, the sound of silence, the humming buzz of "OM." Sound and hearing go together, and both require the element of air. Air is life. Its qualities help us with freedom to express our truth, the flow of easy and nonviolent communication, movement through and around everything. It is untethered, lacks boundaries, is adaptable. Within the cosmic breath is sound vibration, through which we are all connected. The whispering of your heart invites you to reveal your soul, tempting you to find the connection to something even greater.

Your evolution as a divine being does not ever stop, even when you find wholeness. This is a good thing. You can live happily ever after in a state of blissful giving and receiving on the three-dimensional, material plane – it is actually a *must* for humans to thrive. But you can also listen for the secret messages of the universe, hear the whispering of the angels and ascended masters, tune in to the creativity of the gods and goddesses in the archetypal realm, and express your own song of the soul out into the cosmic amphitheater. The glorious wonderment of the voice of the Great Goddess Creatrix wants you to dance with and contribute to this symphony. Your tune, your message, your resonance, your signature sound is vital to the richness of the Cosmic Song.

A message from Rumi came to me during another celestial ceremony of sound healing. There was chanting and music and the natural noises of people clearing their throats, breathing, and shifting into comfort. It was late in the evening. It took me a while to hear the sounds exaggerate with intensity, but I became attuned to the transcendental frequencies. A chime sounded like an echo to infinity, a hiccup landed as the perfect accent, the cacophony of simple human (but normally irritating) sounds were a series of flawless notes contributing to the melody. Breathing was the harmony that connected everyone. That is when Rumi's voice whispered to me, "Sounds create the words, that create the songs, that create the melody, that creates the cosmic symphony that unites us all."

When I am looking for soul guidance, I will ask my question out loud and listen for the answers. Sometimes it is through a song that comes on the radio at the perfect time, the lyrics giving me resolution. Other times it will be a distinct sound or voice in my head. My clairaudient skills are not so refined yet, but the electromagnetic wavelengths called radio waves are how everyone can hear the celestial messages. If you have ever had a song pop into your head, even if there was no music playing, take it as a sign that your guides are trying to communicate with you. If a song sticks in your head, pay attention to the lyrics and how they make you feel. Sound, breath, and vibration are ways that the Universe and her many spirit guides try to communicate with us.

The power center located at the throat is called the *Vishuddha* chakra. It is the center of communication, creativity, and authentic expression. With this power center activated, we can communicate with others, express our truth, and listen deeply. We take the creative impulse and energy of the sacral chakra and move it to this center as inspired creation out in the world. We must own our truth, live our truth, and express our truth. We do this by being aware of the lower vibrations. We take responsibility by owning them, transforming them, and integrating them, which we've already done. Then we infuse the energy with unconditional love from the heart center and elevate it to the throat chakra for creative expression. You can tell if your throat chakra is out of alignment, as you or others will mirror this imbalance with gossip, invalidation, blame, or judgment. You might also feel like your throat gets tight whenever you want to speak your truth, or you get cut off mid-sentence.

The goddess that rules speech, communication, and creativity is Saraswati from the Hindu tradition. Iris is the Roman goddess of the rainbow that served as messenger to the Olympian gods, while Bath Kol is the angel of prophecy and heavenly voice, who offers profound insights into the future. I like to invoke these goddesses of the cosmos to help keep me in my truth and integrity, to receive the messages when I meditate for inspiration, when I create out in the world through my writing, photography, movement practice, designing, or creating ritual and ceremony. They, and my personal set of guides, assist me when I conduct Soul Sessions with my clients. A Soul Session is the evocation of personified energies within a person and offering them a voice. This is another effective way to learn about the many facets of your being, and give them life.

When I work with the throat chakra, many clients have described their blocks with sensations like "it seems like my throat has been slit," "I'm convinced in a past life I was hanged," "It feels like someone has their hands around my throat."

I had the privilege of doing a Soul Session with an exquisite celestial soul sister named Ricquel. Ricquel, a business school graduate working at a nine-to-five desk job, was having a hard time finding her true passion and purpose. During our session, we discovered three different inner personas competing for expression. She named them Diane, Nancy, and Beulah. Diane came forth as a magical and creative ally, which animated Ricquel in a vibrant way. Although Ricquel always felt this energetic presence, her inner Diane "told" her that she stepped back from her creative force sometime in preschool to appease the overbearing teachers. The persona of Nancy came forth as the wild girl who loved to party, have sex, and did not care about what anyone thought about her. She revealed that she was activated to protect Ricquel from feelings of emotional shame and the pains of her experience being raped in college. This was her modified act of rage. Finally, when her inner Beulah revealed herself, Ricquel's body slumped into an apathetic posture. Ricquel described her as a drag. Beulah expressed that she needed to step in to tame Nancy and protect Ricquel from Nancy's recklessness. With the confusion of these competing energies, Ricquel couldn't figure out how she wanted to serve others.

After we gave voice to these energetic personas, and made agreements to who was really in charge – which would be the true essence of Ricquel who is connected to the cosmic space of infinite possibilities – we learned that Ricquel wanted to be a healer and guide for rape victims. Diana would be the energy she called upon to help her intuitively create in the world. Ricquel's journey is now unfolding with more clarity and meaning.

In addition to calling on archetypal deity energies for help, calling on your inner personas will shift your blocks into forces that support you. Soul Sessions are a way to help separate and get to know the many personalities that you have within your being, and give them voice so that you can begin to express your truth with more awareness and authenticity.

If you have ever felt that you lost your creative inspiration, or your self-expression has been blocked, you can also call on the goddesses to help discover when this blockage happened, and to liberate it through a process of recapitulation and ritual to open your throat chakra. Because the color blue represents this power center, you can use a blue-colored crystal or stone such as turquoise for its positive and creative properties of communication and expression.

In a quiet room, sit with your sits bones evenly balanced and your spine lifted in an upright position. Try to relax as much as possible. If you can, keep your right foot flat on the floor and your left foot on your toes with the heel up, as if you were wearing a stiletto. An experienced intuitive medium taught me this foot position as an energetic opening to the spirit world. Try it with both feet flat on the ground to feel the difference, and choose which you prefer. You can keep your left palm opened upward on your lap, while holding the turquoise in your right palm. Ask Bath Kol for inspiration, and Iris to clear the airwaves for you. Take a deep nourishing breath in for four counts and fill up your lower belly until it fills the chest, hold it for four counts, release it for four counts, and then hold your breath for four counts. Do this four times. This type of breathing exercise is used by U.S. Navy Seals, meditators, athletes, and anyone who wants to reduce stress and increase concentration. This breath stimulates the vagus nerve, which branches out to many parts of the body for self-regulation and healing, ultimately producing a calm and relaxed feeling in the mind and body. And, as an added bonus, the 4444 sequence is an angel number saying you are profoundly supported.

You can say this mantra out loud, *"om aim saraswati namaha,"* to invoke the goddess Saraswati for guidance as you tap into your truth and go backward in time to find when your throat chakra might have closed. As you repeat the Saraswati mantra a few times, you can visualize her as a beautiful woman wearing the color white, for purity, as she sits on a white lotus flower. She holds a small lute on her lap, and you notice a white swan beside her.

Then go backward in time and begin to think about what you were doing a day ago. Go back further to the time you decided to read this book. Then go back even further. What were you doing a year ago? Go back to your first job as an adult. If you were a college or postgraduate student, filter through the years to a significant time that you can remember. Return to high school graduation, and then go back through middle school. Remember when you were fourteen, then twelve, then eleven. Go further back still, to seven, then five, then three. If you would like, take yourself back to the womb space. Do this exercise with your eyes closed. Oftentimes our throats will feel tight at a certain timeframe, even if we haven't visualized a specific event. Meditate on the situation to discover if there was a specific event or clues that stopped you from sharing your truth.

For practical use, when we liberate our voices and own our truth, we can communicate with consciousness. Conscious communication includes observing and stating the facts of the situation, and affirming the person you are speaking with by validating their experience and letting them know you hear them. Then identifying the feelings you are going through and removing any blame for them while expressing your needs and the needs of your communication partner. Finally, discussing boundaries and how you want things to happen. The reality of this three-dimensional plane is that each person has the free will to walk their individual path of evolution at their own pace. You will most likely be confronted by those who are uncomfortable with your fabulosity and you will want to "broadband" your energy and use the practical skills of communication with those who might want to challenge your growth. This makes it easier to start co-creating with the Universe.

Your personal creative expression and authentic voice are the kiss of the Cosmic Breath. It is crucial to the individual soul, and to the collective experience of soul awakening and ascension. As our consciousness expands, it is in the story of *you* that feeds everything else. It is the story of *you* that creates the perfect pattern in the tapestry of life. Your authenticity is the very thing that adds life and variety to this great big world.

{*Lesson: Your authentic expression is a gift to the Cosmos.*}

The Cosmic Mind

"Faith, consciousness, and awareness
all exist beyond the thinking mind."
—Ram Dass

Before the word, was the thought. Welcome to your cosmic mind. This is the third eye chakra, or the space where the pineal gland exists in the center of your brain. Ether is the ruling element in this chakra. While the eyes may be the window to your soul, they see the material world in only three dimensions. The third eye is capable of seeing beyond the three-dimensional world into other dimensions, and to Source itself. It is the human galactic portal into divine space.

When our third eye chakra is closed, we might experience anxiety, depression, and loneliness. Of course, all animals will experience anxiety if there is a looming danger about, and many, of course, will continue to experience PTSD from unhealed past traumas. Sacred anxiety, the feeling of being disconnected or alone in your spiritual experience, is the longing to feel divinely connected. It is the soul's yearning to remember the expansive and blissful feelings of Source energy before we came into this dense planet to learn. This is why we yearn for soul-connected love.

An open third eye is the portal to cosmic magic: telepathy, the Clair senses, astral travel, and other paranormal activity. Through this portal we can commune with our Higher Self and the Higher

Selves of others and interact with Higher Guides like the gods and goddesses you've already met from the archetypal realm who are waiting so patiently to share their sacred wisdom through you.

Ancient cultures taught that we can achieve freedom by holding the duality of this material realm alongside the Reality (with a capital R) of the multidimensional Universe. Awakening of the third eye is essential to spiritual fifth-dimension connection, and living an extraordinary three-dimensional life, *at the same time*. We see things in a more holistic way from this cosmic vantage point.

There are many ways to awaken the pineal gland, like the breathing experiences of holotropic and yogic breath, meditation, and of course psychedelics. If you want to live a responsible and social life, you can't live in the stars only (this is a message for those of you who would rather leave your bodies and only play beyond the atmosphere). The way to embody this experience of the multidimensional world is to bring these images, feelings, thoughts of love, and this transcendental magic back into the body. We are souls having a human experience *in the body*, so we might as well enjoy this embodied experience while we are here.

Your connection to Source turns into a thought. That thought becomes word. Those words distill in your heart to become *you*. How you give and receive becomes your action through the solar plexus. When you activate more creativity and desire, then root your intentions into the earth, it is translated into form. This form is experienced, and flows back up through the power centers of our physical bodies for refinement, and back down again to create a continuous rebirth of expression and refinement of embodied experiences and wisdom. This expansive breath of life from your third eye into your body breaks the bonds of the egoic mind to become liberation in the cosmic mind.

This connection creates the radiance of our auric field. When you meet someone with a "great aura about them," they have a fluid connection with the earth, the body, and the cosmos. You become bigger and brighter, and, yes, sexier, because it is naturally magnetic. A quick reminder, your *Beingness* is divine, so you will receive what is divinely required for that level of being. If you are epic love in the flesh, you will receive what is required for epic love. If you are the embodiment of inspiration, you will continue to be inspired by the world around you. If you are fully empowered, you will inherit greater gifts that enhance your power. This is the Cosmic Law of Being.

As I've described earlier, the space of no-thing is the place of pure potential. It exists in the outer reaches of the universe where the elements are still unborn, as well as the place within your soul that is eternally void, where dreams, hopes, and desires are first inspired. This is where we incubate our ideas with the wisdom of Consciousness. This no-place is at the center of the cosmic mind. To clarify, the "mind" is not just the brain. The mind is the intelligence of the heart and other organs, the gnostic body, cellular memory, emotional intelligence, plus all the information of the gut microbiome ecosystem (now considered a second brain) in our stomach that transmits information to the brain in seconds. It is the psyche and the etheric body. The cosmic mind is the integrated intelligence of your entire system, plus the information of the Akashic field, another word for the eternal void beyond space and time that is both nothing and everything.

This place of emptiness in the cosmic mind is the birthplace of all creation, universal and material, which is why meditation has proven to be so valuable not just for stress, but for the creative impetus. In the 99.99 percent of the unknown universe, creation is happening all the time. Stars burst into existence from the "no-place" place. It is the same within ourselves, and why I'll suggest a meditation practice here. During meditation, the space between your thoughts (the gap), is exactly like the 99.99 percent of creative dark energy from which universes and galaxies erupt.

After my soul awakening and my subsequent research on the topic, I decided to investigate and explore the sacred aspects of psychedelics (which might have to wait for a different book), because so many spiritual leaders have also explored these substances. I did not feel like I could fully understand what was going on with me spiritually without exploring what Ram Dass, Timothy Leary, Steve Jobs, The Beatles, and even current spiritual leaders, who have not yet publicly shared their experiences with psychedelics, had experienced. I am not a recreational drug user in any way, and I did have my personal judgments about medicine journeys. As a bona fide soul seeker in stilettos though, I felt it an obligation to study and experience something that I had a slightly negative opinion about (and yes, I'm also as curious as a cat).

I was introduced to "the toad" by a shaman in Northern California. She came highly recommended through the secret channels of the elite explorers on the subject. By elite I mean medical professionals, scientific researchers, and medicine journey healers who study the effects of psychedelic medicine journeys as an underground practice. 5-MEO-DMT is the technical name for "the toad" – it is supposed to be much stronger than DMT, which you may have heard of, but with greater intensity in a much shorter time frame. DMT is a hallucinogenic tryptamine element that appears naturally in a variety of plants (like magic mushrooms) and animals. There is some evidence, according to *Medical News Today*, that DMT is also produced naturally in the pineal gland of the brain. It is sometimes referred to as the "spirit molecule."

When I began speaking with the shaman who would guide me on my toad experience, I started to feel it working before I even met her. Over the phone, I told her how I felt like my body was already eager and flexible as waves of love endorphins rushed over me. She told me that this substance "was God," and of course She was working with me already. As DMT is considered the "spirit molecule," 5-MEO-DMT is considered "the God molecule." As I searched for more information, one experienced toad explorer shared her intense experience of her ego being ripped apart from her body, while another seeker said she felt like she had died, gone to Heaven, and came back. From the research I had done, all the experiences were profound and healing. I was really excited and scared to meet God.

I arrived at the shaman's very small office surprised to see a petite, quiet, and beautiful young woman. I was expecting a very old and wise barefooted High Priestess, wearing a Hare Krishna robe. This healer was in jeans and a t-shirt. I didn't know if I was going to lick a frog or be bitten by one (clearly not enough research!). After our greetings, she pulled out a glass vapor pipe and explained the process. We tested a little bit first to give me a felt sense of what to expect. With trepidation, I inhaled what looked like crystals, and briefly felt like a crack junkie. It was not lost on me that I had just breathed in the misty essence of dried venom from a toad prophet. After our test run, it was time for the real dosage. She sat me on the bed, added the perfect amount of crystals to the vapor pipe, and instructed me to take another big inhale and hold my breath. I did as I was instructed. In a flash, an intense surge pushed me backward, as the shaman said it would, and I felt my head fall onto the soft pillow. She must have put an eye mask over my eyes, because I woke up with one on.

Unexpectedly, I felt a blissful feeling envelope my whole body, and I smiled. I saw incredible imagery undulate in my mind's eye. I saw Fibonacci circles swirl in and out of shape, and ancient mandalas dancing in a kaleidoscope of intense colors. It all happened so very quickly, too quickly for me. Then all of a sudden, I found myself in this place of emptiness. I was aware that there was nothing all around me, only a black void. No dust, no gravity, no flicker, no sense, no nothing. It felt like nothing, it looked like nothing, it tasted like nothing, it sounded like nothing. I was consciously aware of nothing. It is really hard to describe what "nothing" is like.

I felt like my eyes were open with simple curiosity about this nothingness. I had no fear. I had a brief thought that maybe this was death, but that was too simple a thought. Still, I was not afraid. It was just nothing. Then I thought, maybe this was the gap, the place of no-thing, the place of infinite possibilities. That thought felt right somehow, and I surrendered to this emptiness until I got a little bored with it, actually. A piece of wisdom I received at the moment of my boredom was to be curious over fearful. If I tried to control the experience or be fearful, I would see my own demons. It was a choice; it is always a choice. I learned that a youthful, innocent curiosity triumphs over fear. We can receive a great deal of healing, and profound wisdom can be gained by allowing our experiences to unfold with detached curiosity.

I realized that I could create anything I wanted to create. But what would be the most appropriate thing to first create out of nothing? I didn't know. The very second I doubted myself, I witnessed instant grey fog. Every time I said to myself, "I don't know what to create," even more dense fog appeared. I heard myself, or maybe I was guided, to just choose anything, as I could course correct whenever I wanted to. There were no right or wrong answers here, just choices. At that very instant, a prism of colors and shapes danced and shifted forms in my mind's eye; there were infinite expressions. I saw in technicolor the vibration of artisan, inventor, sculptor, writer, musician, and more; I felt them, too. It was really beautiful. I understood then that what we pay attention to is created instantly, and if we are aware of this and add more intention to our attention, we create what we desire.

I don't know what happened after that. The medicine is only supposed to last twenty minutes, but it felt like eternity in a few crystals. As I lay on the bed for another hour or so, I saw a bit of my future and felt the impact of knowing that I would need to let go of the old energies I was clinging on to before my new empowered life could begin. I got up smiling to the thought that God is a toad, and I say that with reverence.

I share this story because I learned that manifestation is actually creation using the Law of Intention and Desire. Intention and attention are the ingredients that energize your desires into a cosmic momentum that pulls all the necessary elements together for your thoughts to manifest into form. Where attention goes, energy flows; this is the artistry of desire. Intention is the real power behind the desires *that you are ready for*. This is a very important distinction. Your energy might be calling out for "the epic love you deserve," but your inner wounds might fear you into believing that you are undeserving of such love. This conflicting message is what you are going to get to challenge your very worth. Your higher self and the guides surrounding you want you to get clear so that your deepest, most authentically-aligned desires trigger the Universe to organize circumstances and people around your refined desire so that it manifests *with ease and grace.* Attention and intention brings about conscious transformations. When we sit in limbo, we sit in a dense fog of unknowing.

When I meditate on the experience, I always get greater wisdom from it. I understand that we all have the God/Goddess seed of potential in us, and we are creating our realities all the time, in such magnificent ways. I learned that fear is such a waste of time, and following your bliss and your passions with unconditional love is what matters the most. You can never get anything wrong; everything is simply an experience to learn from. So stop judging yourself and others. Once you taste, feel, hear, see, smell such divine profundity, you cannot unknow it. We can go to this place whenever we want, and you don't have to experiment with psychedelics to do so. You can take time to meditate, asking your critical mind to quiet and your ego to take a long vacation so there is more space between your thoughts. Your peak performances are examples of harnessing this zone of potential. We need to learn how to empty ourselves of all desire before we can properly manifest our deepest soul-centered desires.

Tapping into this space of infinite potential, the gap, the space of no-thing, the void, emptiness, as much as you can through meditation aligns you with your true essence, your song of the soul, and to Creation itself.

{Lesson: The Space of Infinite Possibilities
is closer to you than you think.}

The Song of the Soul

"Music in the soul can be heard by the Universe."
—Lao Tzu

I know you can feel it in the air sometimes, the stirring at the center of your soul, when everything seems to be going in the right direction. This is the lightness of being one with the flow of life, with the air and ether elements of the cosmic whole.

If you could follow just one suggestion, I would ask you to choose the whisper of your truest self; hearing Her words as the voice within. Let the sounds of the cosmic song embrace you, take you, and have Her way with you. Let the language of ancient mystery and wisdom be your language. I take the liberty to reinvent a quote from the Gospel of John: "In the beginning was the word, and the word was with Goddess, and the word was Goddess."

Your thoughts are translated into words, and they come from the space of infinite possibilities, of pure consciousness. So incomprehensible is the vast and ever-expanding – and mostly empty – cosmos, that we can be reminded again and again that it holds and contains *everything* that we know and that we don't know. Words cannot describe something this awe-inspiring. We are gifted only our experiences in the world, and this we *can* put into words. We can also put words to our future desires and how we want to feel about them. This is how we co-create with the cosmos. This is what it means to say we are currently in the middle of our stories.

Right now, whether you have just come out of a traumatic experience, or buried it deep down for a long period of time – or maybe you are the fortunate one who has been gifted ease and grace already, but still feel there is something even more luxuriously alive waiting for you – you are in the center of your story that is about to unfold to its miraculous climax. This is the section where we connect the dots of the past chapters and understand our current constellation of being, which tells us a little bit more about how we are meant to live, express, serve, create, and love from a place of wholeness in this lifetime.

Your personal creative expression and authentic voice are essential to the individual soul *and* the collective experience of soul ascension. As our consciousness expands, it is in the story of *you* that feeds everything else, it is the story of *you* that creates the perfect pattern in the tapestry of life, *your* authentic soul is the very thing that adds music and harmony and joy and love to everything in existence. You are meant to be here, you are meant to sing your soul's song, you are meant to create your desires, you are meant to love.

Everything in the universe vibrates a song, a noise, a music, a knowing. Everything that vibrates out into the universe permeates through everything else and connects to All That Is. We are all connected through the song of our souls. Each piece of sand sings the sand song, birds sing a bird song, trees have a tree song, rocks have the rock song. The combination of nature's sound vibrations creates the music of praise to the Cosmic Creatrix. The only sound on earth that isn't an authentic sound of *being* comes from humans. This information was downloaded from my sorcerous soul sister Patty, who can hear sound vibrations. We can witness this in nature just by noticing that the trees are just being trees, as the ocean is just being the ocean. Humans seem lost sometimes, our sound is not of *being*, but of yearning. It sounds like a collective hum of mourning.

Everyone knows the feeling of yearning. Yearning is the incorrect song for us. Patty describes that sound like a fish swimming out of the water grasping for life, but not realizing that it is actually in the water. The fish wants to go someplace else for that feeling of comfort and connection. We humans are like that fish, unaware that we are already swimming in an ocean of divinity. This song of simple praise from all of nature is extremely beautiful, which adds to the symphony of the cosmos. We are asked to reconnect to our *beingness* to contribute to the cosmic song. When we learn to plug back into that loving vibration, the sound is pure and the earth raises her vibration too.

How do we fine-tune the yearning into the sound of yummy satisfaction, glorious fulfillment, delightful pleasure, exquisite comfort, passionate actualization? It is to know the self, the multidimensional self, the personified energies from the root, sacral, solar, heart, throat, and third eye chakra, and what each persona from these energy centers desires. As we move up the chakra system and integrate each, we connect to Source through the crown chakra. Avatars are the animation of these power centers, their images help the critical mind to move aside and allow the magical mind to influence your nervous system to create a lush landscape for you to heal and thrive in. When you tap in to our divine self, your individual soul no longer yearns, she sings the song of Being. The Goddess wants to hear your song. This is an act of courageousness that exists through divine feminine wisdom.

{*Lesson: Everything that exists in the great big Universe is waiting to hear your song.*}

Cosmic Creatrix

"There was something undefined and complete,
coming into existence before Heaven and
Earth… formless…reaching everywhere and
in no danger of being exhausted. It may
be regarded as the Mother of all things."
—Tao Te Ching

We weirdos, provocateurs, sacred rebels, visionaries, and cre-atrixes push the edge of the profound and the profane to shake up the predictable closeminded attitudes and exclusive systems of patriarchal rule. We disrupt outdated ideas, unleash waves of repressed emotions, and open up the portals of creative genius. We think about things in a different way, so that new and vibrant worlds can explode into existence. We are the storytellers, the poets, the artists, and the musicians and the dancers who dare to dive deep into the soul in order to make beautiful our collective fears, guilts, shames, should-haves, and resentments. We turn wounds into glorious masterpieces. We tell the truth in our own authentic way.

Everyone is a Creatrix; we are creating all the time. But most women don't believe in this inherent gift, dismissing the qual-ity and artistry of life to focus on the material quantities in life. As innocent curious children, we were so much closer to the collective space of inspiration, because we didn't have any rules or blocks to stop us. I invite you to be curious again. Let's adopt the beginner's mind when it comes to creativity, and dissolve

the veil of illusion here and now. Let's use the life-force energy
you discovered in the sacral womb of creation and bring it up
to the throat chakra so that you can co-create with the universe,
and understand how to manifest your desires with even greater
finesse. It is your soul's purpose to create, but what you create
is up to you.

The two places we source creative energy are in the collective realm, and the deep wisdom of the body in the womb space.
In this book, we have been tapping into Creative and Visionary
Consciousness already. The myths and legends of the goddesses
in this archetypal realm mirror our inner experience. The common legendary myths show us the battle we wage internally, and
therefore out into the world unconsciously. Creative energy is
the inherent animating force within us and in the universe. This
energy elevates our stories to that next level. Through this creative life force, we express our genius. Remember, feminine energy
is nonlinear and creative, while masculine energy is linear and
scientific. Einstein wrote, "Imagination is more important than
knowledge," and, "knowledge is limited, imagination encircles the
world." As I see it, genius requires non-linear, creative thought;
therefore, you already exude feminine genius. Own it.

The primordial energies that dwell beneath the surface of your
being in the sacral chakra have been described as polarity, the
electromagnetic pulse, the sexual life-force energy, or Kundalini.
Once unleashed and fully expressed, you can tap into the creativity sourced from your inner wisdom and mix it with the wisdom
of the cosmos. The elements of creative genius are your body
impulses of desire, hunger, and need; your energetic impulses of
passion and pleasure; the dynamic tension of polarity; the fluid
exchange of penetrating and receptive ideas; and the orgasmic

release of focused inspiration. Genius comes when you accept the "death" of your creation, meaning you need to let it go. This is surrender to the circle of life.

These five cosmic creativity phases help you make certain your creations align with your true essence. Let's practice by thinking about something you'd like to create. The first stage is to make sure your idea is aligned in the "dream realm" of no structure. Here is an example, "I want to share with the world how to live authentically with purpose and passion," or "I want to be love in the flesh." This is the stage of conception. Don't do anything but imagine what you would like to create. If you want to call on Saraswati, Bath Kol, or Iris to help you open up your third eye, do this now. The archetype of the enchantress teaches us about Creation and our power to co-create and birth into being what has never existed before.

The next phase is the gestation phase, when your bigger idea must be put into a thought *form*. "I will write a book about this," or "I will create an easy system that helps me embody love wisdom." How do you want this idea to manifest? Have you had desires to speak publicly, author a novel, create a business or product that helps you and others? Do not worry if you want to make music and you aren't a musician, just focus on the more precise form.

Next, you go into labor. This is when your idea is manifesting into a three-dimensional form by planning, talking about it, starting the process of writing. You already have a journal partially filled with important information about your hopes and dreams and superpowers; you can pull inspiration from here. Some of you are at this phase now and just need to make sure that all your creativity is aligned with your essence and your desires to progress with ease and grace. This stage can take months or even years, depending on what you are creating. It took me about four years to write and publish my first book, and four months, during the 2020 COVID-19 pandemic lockdown, to write and publish this second book.

The next phase is your ecstatic birth, when your idea is actually brought to earth and serves the planet and humanity in some way. This is the published copy of your book, the painting on the wall, the new love affair with yourself or with another. It's important to include gratitude for your efforts, and for all the cosmic magic and collaboration that helped you create this masterpiece.

Finally, your transformation or the transformation of others is the death cycle phase. You let go of what you created and start again at a new level of growth. You can write a second book, or include a workshop. You can create more romance in your life, or start a family. There is always room for creation, whether it is upgrading your system or creating something entirely new.

It's now time to step into the role of Creatrix. She is beyond receiving material rewards or accolades for privileged education, she is all about you and your knowing. We all have the opportunity to teach ourselves through our experiences. If we only take the word of the gurus who simply regurgitate the texts they've studied, versus embodied, the teachings are still a concept. The gift of each of your experiences, in the shadow realm or in the light realm, is that you know it, you have felt it, you were transformed by it, and now you sparkle with it. This personal experience makes you the expert on *you*. No cookie cutters here, just pure potentiality and absolute creativity.

All the blocks and shadow energies that we had discovered in the root and sacral chakras are your juicy, tantalizing, mesmerizing elements that make your life the story worth living. We can take anger or anxiety and channel it into something creative; in fact, that is the transformational process. It is another way to release them as blocks. These truths are part of your soul's song and, when put together and seen from a higher perspective, you will realize what an amazing story of life you wrote for yourself in the world between the worlds.

You might not have realized it, but you have gained all the tools you need to finish writing the rest of your epic adventure, and to include your cosmic magic to the unified field of consciousness. Now is the time to finish writing the rest of your epic tale. We are going to tap into our creative right brain, and give space to the voice within by limiting the left brain's desire to correct and analyze. You will need your journal and a timer.

Your Soul has a purpose and a voice that wants to be unleashed. We are going to find out what she has to say. To do this, you will need to put away all distractions and simply think about your future self, who has transformed all the lessons she needs to find her truth. You do not need to look through your journal; trust that what is important has stayed with you. Get your timer out and set it to one minute. In sixty seconds, write the title of your whole life's story (including the future that you haven't yet lived), plus a few sweeping phrases about your legacy. There is no wrong way to do this. Simply trust that your magical mind is capable of expressing words, feelings, and images that the left brain will want to edit. Do not worry about spelling or grammar, just jot down as many notes as you can. When your timer stops, please stop.

Your critical mind would like to edit what you just wrote, but we are going to continue with the magical mind. Set your timer now for three minutes. When you are ready – and remember not to analyze too much – for the three minutes, list fifteen memorable themes on your life's journey so far and those yet to come. Again, there is no right or wrong, just whatever comes to your mind.

Set your timer for another three minutes. Don't focus too much on this, but I am reminding you now that you have already envisioned what your Eden would look like and what your instinctive animal powers are, you have witnessed the shadow realms, know your sacred weapons of truth, and understand that you are a divine spark of light that is already tapped into the cosmic womb of Creation. You've already written down your desires. Do not yet put down this book! You are primed right now to turn to a blank page in your journal, start the timer, and for three minutes, yes, only three minutes, write down your whole story from start to your future miraculous climax. Ready, set, go.

{Lesson: You're not at the climax of your epic tale.
Your future is still open wide to suggestions.}

CHAPTER 9
Almighty Goddess

The Golden Shadow
You are Stardust
Almighty Goddess

The Golden Shadow

"Our deepest fear is not that we are
inadequate, our deepest fear is that we are
powerful beyond measure. It's our light,
not our darkness that most frightens us.
We ask ourselves who am I to be brilliant,
gorgeous, talented, fabulous."
—Marianne Williamson

Within each dark shadow of our soul is a gleaming golden light of potential. You have already learned that there are both shadow and light aspects of the whole. This is duality, and there is choice in duality. What would it mean to shine brighter than the Sirian star, to be as radiant as the sun, to be more luminous than the moon? Do you really believe that there is a soul out there that perfectly resonates with and brilliantly loves your own soul? Could you even handle such freedom in this kind of love? How responsible would you be if you embodied such great powers? Would you use them for good, or for selfish reasons? What if you were asked to lead others, would you be up for the task? These are the sneaky little whispers that our ego mind pulls out at the very last minute, just before we are faced with the choice to step into our own golden light or slink back into the darkness, forcing us to go through the soul refining process once again.

Carl Jung called the disbelief in the luminous aspect of the self the Golden Shadow. We reject and hide our feminine genius, the intelligence of our gnosis, our intuition, our sensuality, our exquisite and unique beauty, our radiant power, our talents, and the love in our hearts. Instead, we project them onto other people so we don't have to accept these gifts as our own.

Even though you've followed the way of the goddess, discovered the magical mystery of you, integrated your superpowers, and are poised to step into the limelight of your own radiance, you might hesitate. In one moment you may think that magic and miracles must be true in you, and the next moment you might question the very existence of the unnamable, eternal, omnipotent, omnipresent, omniscient "OM" of the multiverse. This resistance is your Golden Shadow. I am here to remind you that your very existence is a miracle that proves there is divine order in this great cosmic playground. If you cannot fully accept the golden light of miracles and magic in you, how can you accept this presence in anyone or anything else?

You might be wondering why it so hard to step into the light. It's because of your unconscious fear of being forever disconnected to Divine Love. When our souls first entered this planet, we immediately felt the separateness from All That Is. We interpret the feeling of separateness as rejection, which creates the urgent need to bond in relationships and feel part of a community. We will do things just to fit in, like sell our souls, stay small, and remain unconscious. Our unique spark of light is threatened further, because we feel that individuation separates us even more from the incredible unity we felt in the celestial worlds. It has taken many lifetimes for human consciousness to rise to this moment, when more and more people like you are beginning to understand the divinity in everything. Unfortunately, we are still reacting to the mass consciousness of lower-vibrational fear-based energy. But the good news is, once a critical mass of people like you awaken to the truth of who you really are, the darkness manifested as hate crimes, wars, and oppression will no longer be a part of collective consciousness, or at least it won't exist with such enormity on this planet. This requires a great deal of capacity, honesty, trust, surrender, integrity, and humility, and it often feels like too big a task to be Divine and a divinely-guided member of the Light Brigade. You, my soul sister, were born for this sacred mission, and you need only to focus on the most important being on the planet, you. Your only assignment, if you choose to continue to take it, is to be who you really are – a straightforward, simple, but not so easy task.

Don't stop now. Be brave. Keep on rocking your karmic runway. Allow yourself to witness this precious moment of doubt. When the Hall of Mirrors is smashed into pieces, and you no longer search outward for validation, who are you really? When you've dismantled your fears and learned to love fully, what do you desire now? When your shadow archetypes have transformed into their light, what is your soul's purpose now? And when the divine guides leave you to reflect and become empty, what are you grateful for now?

From the very beginning, you heard the eternal call, and you listened to Her song. You caught a glimpse of a dazzling, radiant light, and you looked toward its brilliance. You were transported by a sublime scent of life-force energy, and you inhaled deeply. You tasted the lips of the Divine, and yearned to continue this heavenly kiss. You felt the rapture of cosmic love, dancing through your body and tickling your skin, and you opened to feel even more. When the dark shadows dissolved to reveal your golden light, and you've seen the heavenly rays, what is left? Now you understand that individual sparks of divine spirit, are souls in a human body. Now what?

Believe.

Believe that your individuality, your artistry, your truth, your specialness is your strongest connection to Source. The people who tell you that you are not special are innocently misguided. The very nature of your existence is divine, therefore you are way more than special, as all forms of life are equally special no matter how conscious or unconscious, or how loving or fearful.

This last pearl of wisdom is the only truth you've ever needed. Your connection to Source, the Almighty Goddess within, is your secret weapon, special sauce, and uber-charged divine feminine superpowers. Believe it.

{Lesson: You are so very special.}

You Are Stardust

"It is not so much that you are within the
Cosmos, but that the Cosmos is in you."
—Meher Baba

You are stardust, literally. If you remember from biology class, the most crucial and fundamental elements that allow life to exist on this planet are carbon, hydrogen, nitrogen, oxygen, phosphorus, and sulfur, otherwise known as "the building blocks of life." Astronomers have discovered a bounty of evidence that shows the fundamental elements for human life also exist in hundreds of billions of stars in our Milky Way galaxy. "Inside stars, a process takes place called nucleosynthesis, which is basically the making of elements," says scientist Dr. Ashley King in a *Natural History Museum* article. We humans, and our star sisters in *this* galaxy, have about 97 percent of the same kinds of atoms that are prevalent the closer they get to the galactic center. Deepak Chopra says we were made in the "crucible of stars," and the atoms creating different parts of our bodies could have come from the atoms of different galactic systems. I did mention that a small percentage of my 23andMe DNA screening was "unknown," and considered it to be extraterrestrial stardust. Now I *know* that I'm all stardust, and so are you. The reason why this is so exciting is it adds another dimension to your divine feminine superpowers and expands your celestial realm even farther.

For my sister horoscope geeks, when we know ourselves to be an integral part of the cosmic landscape, we can use the influence of our astrological constellations (based on our birth charts) to guide us on our journey, not tell us what we are doomed for. The planets, stars, and asteroids have archetypal energies that we can work with, not be worked by. For example, the asteroid Lilith has the same influence as our wild woman archetype, Pallas Athena has the same wisdom and temperament as the goddess Athena, and the planet Venus is associated with romance, beauty, and pleasure, just like our goddess from the foamy sea. When you know that you are stardust, you transcend the fateful outcome of your constellation and start using their higher-octave meaning to serve your soul's desires and purpose, and to co-create your future. This is sacred free will in action.

It is worth repeating scientific knowledge in the context of magic, or rather using the language of science to interpret magical reality. If 97 percent of our body consists of the six elements listed above, and everything in the visible universe is made up of atoms, which are made up of the three tiny subatomic particles known as protons, neutrons, and electrons, then everything is energy and information in a constant exchange with each other. From the many lectures I've attended, where Quantum Physicists mingle with Spiritualists, I learned that the microscopic electrons and protons disappear into *probability waves* if you are not paying attention to them, or if they aren't in communication with other particles. What does this mean? Those waves exist non-locally, in the space of no-thing, waiting for the thought, desire, impetus to be manifest into form. The mysteries of the universe are grand, and since you are part of that miraculous creation, you are a miracle too. In fact, you are the Cosmos, and have the ability to shift your awareness to reveal how the Real you is capable of creating magic and miracles.

Speaking about superstars and divine light, the interpretation of the seven rays is included in many ancient esoteric, religious, and occult philosophies. It was first mentioned in the ancient sacred Vedic texts, where specific rays of light are said to be located in the hidden power chakras in the body. These are the power centers we have been activating together. In Christ Conscious theology, these are the rays that reflect the energies of the angels and Archangels. I was introduced to another description of the seven rays through esoteric philosophy and the esoteric astrologer William Meader, whose lineage is from Ageless Wisdom teachings and the work of esoteric philosopher Alice Bailey. Her book *The Seven Rays of Life* is a compilation of extracts from many of her other books on the topic of the seven rays. Although these rays also correspond to the power centers already mentioned in this book, the esoteric seven rays have their own flavor. Esoteric philosophers claim these particular rays have different energies sourced from the Great Ray of the Cosmic Light, and that each of our souls comes into this planet with just one of these ray vibrations, but our personalities reflect many. For the purpose of your integration, I incorporate these specific rays with the specific vibrations of the goddess archetypes we've already been working with – to help you sparkle even more brightly. I will focus on the rays as personified in each of us. If we are all stardust, we have the potential for all the energies. I blend the rays here, and allow the goddesses to spring forth in a new way. I believe you are now ready to go into your own body's wisdom to determine how the light rays resonate with you at this stage of discovery.

The first ray is known to be the Will of the Divine. It holds the energy of will, power, and purpose to lose the ego self in order to be connected directly with the Divine. This ray is associated with the crown chakra, which exists at the top of your head. I can feel powerful Kali helping us to redeem the Will of the Divine light ray, as her ferocity for truth, slaying the ego, and showing us who we really are is a true act of courage. Our biggest challenge in life is that we deny the connection with the Great Rays of Source energy, and it truly does take every ounce of willpower to let go of our ego selves, and all that we thought we were, and go inside to find that divine connection. As we first learned, Kali is the destroyer of all evil and considered the most powerful of all Shakti incarnations. When she is exalted as "the will," she is the force that evoked your inner power as shadow slayer to hunt down all that blocks you from your divine feminine light. Athena was said to be birthed from Zeus' forehead, just as Kali came from the head of Durga. They both refuse to let you be afraid of your own power. This energy calls up the Sacred Rebels and Shadow Slayers in each of us.

The second ray is the energy of Love-Wisdom, at the heart center of your body. This is the center where the Law of Attraction lives, and is consistent with the abundant, nurturing, unconditional loving goddess energy of Lakshmi, who I also placed in the heart chakra. In this space, as you already have learned, we magnetically pull everything that we love to us. Venus and Aphrodite have this magnetic essence. We are bonded to our service and purpose by love, compassion, and healing. This is Mother Mary's selfless energy as well. This ray expresses as the Love Avatar in us as we contribute to the ascension of the planet and serve humanity through the Law of Love.

The third ray is the energy of Creative Active Intelligence. It is the Holy Spirit and the relationship with surrendering and trusting that divine consciousness will organize itself so that everything will come together in divine order. As mentioned earlier, the Holy Spirit is also known as the divine feminine Sophia Christ. The energy I describe as the cosmic breath, is inspired by the magical mind, to help us express truthfully and reveal divine purpose. According to Neale Donald Walsch, our purpose is to create whatever we want. Third ray energy helps others to learn and develop authentic expressions of ideas, where you look within for inspiration, consistent with the role the cosmic breath provides. The third ray is located in the throat center, where Saraswati, Bath Kol, and Iris can help you sing the song of your soul as a Cosmic Creatrix.

The fourth ray of light is the energy of Harmony through Conflict. This ray produces beauty, harmony, integration, purity, and wholeness to the planet. It is the energy of design and form of the objective world, connecting the polarities with the qualities of adaptation and intuition. This ray is said to be associated with the root chakra, as it is the foundation of our spine, and therefore the foundation of form. Lady Gaia holds the structure of the earth, while Durga protects her. In Eden, the combining of the wild woman archetype in Lilith and the pure virgin archetype in Eve creates the harmony of the whole woman, as is the integration of Adam and Eve back into balance. We are the masons of the new earth looking for harmony, peace, equanimity, equality, and beauty. We are rooted and wild as the Earth Empress with this ray emphasis.

The fifth ray is the energy of Science or Concrete Knowledge. Obviously, these are the scientists and thinkers who help us comprehend the vast and mysterious natural laws. The balance of the higher cosmic mind and the lower vibration of the critical mind is at work here. You are reminded with this ray that you are your own guru. This is the ray of the third eye chakra, where the cosmic mind organizes our thoughts into true form. This is the realm where the goddess Saraswati and Hecate also inspire pure and creative thought, to help your inner Love Alchemist bring thought into form in practical ways.

The energy of the sixth ray is that of Devotion and Idealism. This ray helps us actually see the ideal Reality behind the form, to see beyond the veil into the mysterious and magical realms. The devotional love of the sixth ray is said to be embodied best by Jesus, who is known as the sixth Ray Master in esoteric philosophy. This ray is the energy of the world servers, the light brigade, the stewards of the earth, the Holy Warrioress within you. They are looking for the hidden meaning behind form, by looking for what is false and what is true. Love is truth.

Seventh ray energy is the energy of Magic and Ceremonial Order. This is the sacred dream that unifies our inner qualities and the outer tangible actualized form. It is the divine container that holds and connects the energy in the archetypal realms to influence magic, miracles, and the teaching that all forms are spiritual. "As above, so below. As within, so without," is the unity consciousness motto in this ray. All of the deity archetypes and the elementals are active in this realm to help the Almighty Goddess in all of us dance with the divine, and merge the space between Heaven and Earth.

Now that the rays of light from above are mixing with your individual essence in each power center, I feel the jubilant Shakti of all goddesses channeling her celestial light through me to embrace you and shower you with triumphant love.

Gorgeous, radiant, magical, mystical, powerful, beautiful, sensual soul, can you feel how the prism of all the rays of light enters your cells to activate the whole and the Holy of you? As the luminous and spectacular iridescent golden light that you are, at this very moment, We thank you for the kiss, the whisper, the heartbeat of your exquisite essence. Do not turn back now beloved, your journey toward Divine Love and Light is just beginning.

{Lesson: You are not just stardust, you are everything.}

Almighty Goddess

Beauty, you have entered a portal into a new reality. In this cosmic stratosphere, your divine feminine superpowers and extraordinary goddess qualities are a natural expression of who you truly are. This is a mystical, magical Reality, where both the physical and metaphysical experiences are felt and known simultaneously. It is time for your crowning.

You have experienced your primordial essence as nature's earth, water, fire, air, and ether to know yourself as a reflection of the Earth Empress, feel yourself as this magnanimous energy. You have claimed your sacred space on this planet. As a newly-appointed stewardess of the earth, your primordial gifts are protection, belonging, regeneration. You have activated your elemental powers to ground, flow, ignite, inspire, and let go, so that you embody the rooted and wild feminine who reclaims her spiritual inheritance of the mysteries and powers of the first woman, the Tree of Life, the serpent in Eden. You've learned to look fear in the face and transform it into love. Your rooted power is now activated.

Shift into the energy of the Sacred Sexual High Priestess and Shadow Slayer and reclaim your soul. You dove into the depths of the Ocean of Knowing to awaken your senses and sensual superpowers, understanding that flowing with all your feelings is to be empathic and compassionate with others. To be in touch with your watery soul is the only way to know your desires. You've swum into the dark shadowy caves to find the pearls of wisdom to heal the wounds of shame and guilt for what is inherently and divinely feminine – your sacred sexuality. The shadow slayer in you fear-lessly took on the deadly sins with grace and ease, so you could enter the Womb of Creation and surrender to the fulfillment of your desires. Surrendering to your intimate and most sacred self is the invitation for a divine love to run toward you. Open your soul to what is coming to you. Your sacral power is now activated.

Stand with warrioress stature and own this kind of empower-ment. You ignited your soul fire and entered the sacred Pyramid of Light. Courageously, you found your holy weapons of truth and your innate powers, so you could empower and serve oth-ers with the highest integrity. With your electromagnetic charge amplified, you refined the polarity of your animal instincts and effortlessly achieved Holy Warrioress status. You understand the magic of alchemy and the fire of transformation. Your solar power is now activated.

Fill your heart up with the unconditional love of the Love Avatar. You churned all of your past experiences, merging the powers of the dark and the light just as the demons and devas did to resurrect Lakshmi from the milky waters to restore Paradise in your heart. You rose from the poisons and found yourself in an abundant Heaven on Earth, where only love exists. As an awakened divine feminine creature, you resurrected the divine masculine within your own soul to create equality, harmony, and intimacy through the sacred union of you with you. This complete world within influences the uplifting of the external new world. You smashed the Hall of Mirrors into tiny pieces to be recreated as the diamond seed of your own reflection to become a Love Avatar. Love in the flesh is undeniable, indestructible, unbreak-able, and everlasting. You deserve this, you are this. Your heart power is activated.

Swirl with Cosmic Creatrix magic. You chose to inhale a cosmic breath and open up to the cosmic mind, where co-creation and intuition reign. You entered into the space of no-thing and realized that your individual song of the soul is necessary for the realization that your vibration helps the collective ascend as well. You are an essential. How incredible to know that you are the Cosmic Creatrix in this divine space, right in the middle of your epic love story, a masterpiece in progress, continuing to create the climax of your legend. Your authentic expression power and third eye power are activated.

Before we go on, I'd like to finally introduce you to the Hindu goddesses who will guide us through the infinite, boundless, eternal, and ecstatic dimensions outside of our bodies. Aditi is the deity archetype of cosmic limitlessness and infinite space that connects us all, and Bhuvaneshwari is the deity archetype that embodies the whole universe, giving shape to the creation of the world, offering cosmic wisdom and universal understanding. As you can imagine, the universe is a great big, incomprehensible to the human mind, place. The myths, legends, and metaphors of the goddess archetypes from all philosophies, theologies, and religions help us to access the universal themes and experiences of our quest to know the true Self, to battle the internal beasts, to access the hidden powers that lie within, and ultimately become triumphant in Love and Life (with capital L's). Simply imagine them here with you standing in the upper realm right above your head. Give yourself permission to witness yourself as they see you. Allow them to take you even higher to see not just this moment but all moments as one with no space or time, just limitless potential.

From this higher place of witnessing, just one more gift from goddesses before we part. Aditi and Bhuvaneshwari summon all

the goddesses we have already worked with, and ask them to surround you with love. Feel all of them encircle you with their divine
presence. Though each of them carries a specific essence, they
now merge into one to hold you and comfort you. The magnitude
of this complete and sublime energy, with its variations and subtleties, is Shakti. As one, and as many, they would like to remind
you that you have known this energy for all of your life, and that
your time up in the etheric space is eternal. You have already spent
more time with them in this higher dimension than you have on
this earthly plane, you simply forgot. There are no mirrors here,
just you and them. They are asking you to let go of needing their
help at this moment, to trust your magic, and to look just a little
bit deeper. The activation of your divine feminine superpowers
and the claiming and naming of the Almighty Goddess within has
one last action. To simply accept and be *you*.

We could have started and ended with this one very simple
action, but you would not have believed in its simplicity unless
it was masked in the language of constraints and limitations that
humans are so fond of. Humans are resistant to the one thing
they came back to this learning planet to re-member, and that is
Love. You are a spark of angelic light, and a blessed vibration of
the Great Cosmic Goddess-Creatrix, you are connected to All That
Is, you are Love. Your rejection of this Truth is your only issue.
Every obstacle, every block, every shame, every blame, every act
of oppression that you look at and feel the need to transform is
simply a distraction and denial to what you are afraid to admit –
the fact that you are this Divine Love.

{*Lesson: All you have to do is be you.*}

Supercharged Desire Activation and a Final Wish

Supercharged Desire Activation

Congratulations, soul sister! You've solved the mystery of you, and have all the tools to experience self-mastery and self-sovereignty and therefore create and experience life and love as you intended. You know who you are. You are the queen of your earthly world, the divine goddess of your spiritual domain, and every power archetype in between. Now let's go back to where we first met, your desires. Pull out your journal for the last time with me, and look over the pieces of the puzzle that stand out to you. You've practically written your memoir during our time together, and you've definitely activated each of your superpowers. We will do another timed writing exercise based on all you have written and experienced already. Some answers will be the same, while others might have shifted slightly. This supercharged desire activation comes from the clearing of each power center so that your evolved intention can now be planted with more accuracy and purity.

When you are ready, set the timer for twenty seconds for each answer to the following questions, with a pause for breath in between: Who am I? (pause and set timer for twenty seconds) What do I desire? (pause and set timer again) How do I serve? (pause and set timer again) How does my service make others feel? (pause and set timer again) What am I grateful for? (pause and set timer again). Using your refined answers as inspiration, set the timer for one minute and create a desire or purpose statement to include how you will also make others feel, using all positive words. The Universe gives you what you want, so using positive words is a stronger vibration, and She likes it when we give back, too. Do this before you read on.

As each deity archetype has their signature essence, yet all essences come from The Great Cosmic Mother, the Shakti, the Sophia Christ, you too have your signature soul's desire or purpose. Kali came forth with the desire to slay the demons of the ego, to help us find enlightenment. Lakshmi's desire was for beauty in the world, and she rose from the Milky Ocean to bring forth good fortune and abundance for all. You too have a desire that serves yourself and others. Here are a few examples from some incredible souls I've guided through this practice: "I am the divine feminine who brings consciousness to the unconscious through my story of awakening," writes Patricia, a real estate executive who wants to start writing her story to help others heal past wounds. Sam, a single mother of two who just experienced a heartbreak, writes, "I am Love and I am grateful for the experience of the greatest love so that I can guide others toward love." Mary is living in a cramped apartment and is in the process of turning it into a personal retreat. "I am so grateful for this sacred sanctuary where I go to find peace for myself and others." Sarah is an entrepreneur: "I am abundant and deserve to help myself and others secure material wealth in order to give to those who need it most." Ally is a singer and voice coach: "I am a grateful songbird who sings for hope and healing. My song heals the hearts of many." Lola, a grandmother, has a simple desire: "I am grateful for the people in my life and I bring joy to all of them."

Whether you desire to save the world, clean the oceans, make ends meet, or find contentment, when you refine and align your intent and then bring it through the power centers in the body, it becomes part of you. As you will notice, these desires were written from a place of gratitude and as if they already happened. This is key. You can replace "desire" with the word "deserve," if that helps. Remember, when you are an Almighty Goddess, you get what you want. Feel as if your desire has already happened, add gratitude to this energy, and simply rewrite your statement as if it has already happened, and feel the joy it brings. We do this so that you aren't tempted by the needy energy of a desire and hold on to it too tightly. The Universe gives you what you want. If you have the yearning quality attached to your desires, She'll keep you yearning for it. I will change the word desire to deserving as we take your future manifestations through the supercharging process.

Read your deserving statement and then place it in the field of infinite potential. Imagine this place to be a few feet above your head and ask the deities and goddesses in the upper realm for support. Then bring your deserving statement into your Template of Perfection, the blueprint of your highest self that I mentioned earlier, which is about twelve inches from your crown. Then allow your statement to sit as a crown on your head. Feel your deserving statement as a coronation to activate the sovereign self and accept the responsibility of receiving this gift. How does your posture change when your gift is a crown on your head?

Then bring your awareness to your third eye center and see what the outcome of your statement creates. Are people reading your book and smiling? Is your song playing on the radio? Do you see your loved ones laughing together? Are you in a soul-centered relationship? See every detail. See beyond the outcome of your gift to the lineage behind it and ahead. How is your statement rippling through time and space to create something new? The fourth-dimensional guides are busy helping you spread your gift beyond the third dimensional world.

As your deserving statement melts into your throat chakra, listen to the words that you and others say about this gift. Repeat out loud and with conviction the very sentence you created. Sing it, laugh it, say it over, and over again. At the end of your sentence, add, "And may my (add your deserving statement here) manifest with grace and ease, even more spectacular than I can ever imagine. So be it." Do this now and let the vibration echo onto a soundwave to be carried off to the perfect people, places, experiences, and synchronicities. Take a deep breath of life into your deserving statement and exhale its truth.

Allow your deserving statement to drop down into the heart chakra and add an abundance of unconditional love to it. Think of how many hearts you will have touched because your gift is out in the world. Take a moment to purify it in the heart center even more.

Allow your heart's deserving to settle down into your solar plexus, imagining it empowering you and others. This is the time to put fire and passion behind the deserving statement by knowing how to sustain it. Will you write every day? How will you spread love? What is your very next baby step in the doing process? Make sure your gift resonates with you and others still on the material three-dimensional plane. Will people thrive and benefit from the manifestation of your gift?

Then bring your deserving statement into your belly, the sacral chakra, and experience with all of your senses what your manifestation *feels* like. Are you and your partner blissfully in love? What does happiness feel like on your skin? Add all of your positive emotions for yourself and others now, and really feel the luscious sensations. How do the people around you experience their felt senses through your gift? Fill your belly up to bulging with feelings of love and joy and service and ecstasy as you imagine your belly pregnant with this gift, until it swells to the point your pelvic floor feels the heavy weight of your gift ready to be birthed. Imagine you have the security and the relationships and the worthiness for the fullness of your gift and that you will experience a natural and ecstatic birth. Then relax and drop your pelvic floor as if you were allowing this gift to drop like a seed into the earth. Imagine this seed now planted into the earth.

Then let go. The Law of Being requires you to receive everything you need at your level of being. You have been crowned Almighty Goddess, celebrated as Cosmic Creatrix, esteemed as Love Avatar, empowered as Holy Warrioress, revered as Shadow Slayer, restored as Earth Empress and then some. You are beyond worthy of your greatest desire. You can now let go and trust that the Cosmic Laws are at your service. Your job is to come back to earth and make practical progress, but don't ever uncover or replant or dig up the earth to check on it. Continuing with the metaphor, you water it, attend to it, give it sunshine, feed it, and know that your seeds of desire will sprout into your Tree of Life in your Garden of Eden that continuously produces the fruits of wisdom that you need. Let go and trust. I am so excited for you.

A Final Wish

I absolutely enjoyed our time together going deep, getting raw, sharing our naked truth. You are forever a soul sister shining bright with bursts of inspiration for others. The new world we created together is so much better because of your part in it. Thank you for following this golden thread of love and light that has led us to this very moment, where we say goodbye...for now.

The end of every journey always marks the beginning of a new one. This is the grand cycle of life. I cannot wait to know where you are going next. Please know that I am always here for you as your witness and goddess guide to support you as you travel the depths of your soul and back into the light of your divine being. This journey is best done with a compassionate guide who knows the path into the dark and back out into the light.

I encourage you to continue to practice and embody the archetypes that arise for you. Try playing dress up, walking, and posing as each deity so that their energy sinks into your bones. Be photographed as each archetype so you become your own witness to your individual divineness, creating a portfolio of images with recordings of your desires. I do this as an avatar ritual and initiation for all the soul sisters who journey with me in this magical landscape of the Divine Feminine. This magical mind shaping with your own images helps to lock in the body memory of each archetype and superpower, so that your access to each becomes easier and easier. Plus, who wouldn't want to turn into a goddess for a day?

I ask you to be responsible during your interactions with others as you grow and awaken further. You will find, like I did, that your sacred light is blinding to those who refuse to participate in love over fear. But staying true to your core is what allows them to be inspired through love too. Make sure you have a community of Sacred Rebels from the Light Brigade to support you as you learn how to conduct your light.

Please remember that a continuous flow of ritual, witnessing, inspiration, guidance, and a supportive group are essential when traveling the realm of the mystical and magical dimensions, especially in a patriarchal and faux feminine world. As you know now, we do things a little differently. While we are always in collaboration and in relationship with the material world, our language of magic, miracles, myth, and metaphor are often attacked by criticism and rigidity by the linear minds and lower vibration of patriarchal skeptics. This, too, is practice for our highest good.

Always keep in your heart that the goddesses are there for you, and I am too, as your sacred soul guide, translator, and superpower activator as you continue on the path toward enlightenment. I am so grateful for you. My final wish before we go is for you to know without a shadow of a doubt that you are the most exquisite, most spectacular, most delicious divine goddess on this planet...and you are so very loved.

Acknowledgments

I write this book during the 2020 global COVID-19 pandemic lockdown. For me, it is a time of universal and personal introspection, a time when we are all forced to isolate, reflect, review, and decide if we want to be led by fear or love. I have friends who fell sick and survived, friends who had to say goodbye to their elderly parents, and others that were unaffected. I felt the impact of businesses closing, a friend's fear and exhaustion as a frontline worker, and the pain of families struggling to maintain the peace as they fell into the rabbit hole of despair. I also experienced the wave of hope and light and love from the those who see this moment as an opportunity to travel into the portal of change that will bring us to a more gracious, kind, and loving new world. All experiences are valid, honored, and very real. I mention this contrast because it is the very experience of the unknown, the tension that shows us who we are, how we show up, and what we are capable of. I guess I'm also thanking the virus for this time to write. It is my hope that my words inspire you to spread your light and love like a virus that heals the world.

As I write these final words, I must also mention the protests that are erupting all across the United States demanding racial justice, healing, dignity and humanity for Black Lives who have suffered under the brutality of a racist system. A revealing of the vicious shadow side of law enforcement and white privilege. We are all wounded by the pains inflicted on innocent people. I want to thank all of the protesters who validate the need to eradicate fear and hate from this world. We really do need to rise in consciousness and usher in a new world full of peace, harmony and equality for all.

With the creation of this book, I tried to support small business and local artists in my neighborhood. I discovered the artist Joe E. Ladisla, who works as a barista at my local Starbucks. I watched him draw a mermaid on a chalkboard sign when Starbucks finally opened to serve take-out only drinks. I asked him to illustrate a goddess for me. I didn't know he would be that great of an artist. I loved his illustration so much, I used it for the cover of this book. He doesn't have a website yet, but look him up, I hope he gets to continue to draw and create as he intends to. For the inside drawings, I called on make-up artist, Bernadette Szilvas. I've hired Bernadette in the past to transform my clients into goddess archetypes when I photograph them. I noticed that she always sketched ideas before she painted on their faces, but I had no idea what an accomplished painter she was also. Her depth of creativity and magical details are so beautiful to me. You can follow her @bernadette4626. I am grateful for both of these creative geniuses.

I would like to thank my teacher Deepak Chopra and Chopra Certifications for sharing the knowledge of ancient wisdom in a way that I can understand. A great deal of information from my Ayurvedic training at the Chopra Center and the many workshops I attended with Deepak Chopra as teacher, I repurposed here. I also have gratitude for the many teachers who gifted me lessons through the challenges and inspirations in life. I am forever grateful to my late friend Richard Busby, who had awakened me to communicating beyond the veil of perception. Although I was scared shitless at the time (sorry for swearing), I cannot ever forget the eternal magic of his soul. I want to thank the Shaman

Sorceress, Linda, who guided me on some very powerful journeys. She helped me make sense of what was already blossoming inside me. I would also like to thank my "activator," who gifted me that *zing* moment.

Thank you High Priestess, Angela Lauria, for creating this platform. Thank you Warrioress Writer, Bethany Davis, for being the best editor and hand holder on the planet, and many thanks to the rest of the Author Incubator team who helped me publish this book. I am also very grateful for goddess on the rise, Annie Fergus, for being my third eye and for blessing this book with her proofreading prowess.

Finally, I would like to thank my dear friends, especially the Davinistas, and family members who have supported me though some of the most excruciating dark nights of the soul. You know who you are. And of course my guys, who are my heart and soul. I love everything about you.

And I thank you dear reader, for being open and curious and willing.

I am grateful.

Thank You

Beautiful soul sister, I am so grateful and honored to be your guide on this journey. Please keep in touch, the Cosmos always has something up Her sleeve for us! I cannot wait for our next adventure together.

"The Divine in me, bows to the Divine in You."
Namaste

www.lordcoltrane.com
info@lordcoltrane.com
@lordcoltrane

About the Author

Lord Coltrane believes that inside every woman's soul is a confidently beautiful, courageously divine, and consciously sensual feminine essence. Her passion and purpose is to amplify Divine Love and Beauty on this planet. She wants everyone to feel triumphant in love.

Coltrane is a self-proclaimed professional shapeshifter who transforms into visionary artist, soul whisperer, love amplifier, shadow slayer, shame smasher, beauty illuminator, feminine embodiment coach, and spiritual guide whenever such superpowers are needed.

She is a master creatrix at designing ritual and ceremonial experiences to guide women on an archetypal journey and spiritual initiation process inspired by the ancient goddess mystery schools. Her channel to the upper realms is clear and aligned to teach divine feminine wisdom.

Lord Coltrane is a Chopra certified Ayurvedic Educator, Feminine Movement Instructor, Archetype Consultant, Vedic Counselor, accomplished Photographer, and best-selling Authoress. As all starseeds do, she loves to travel and explore the inner and outer worlds. Coltrane lives in California and is madly in love with her family.